Floral
VECTOR MOTIFS

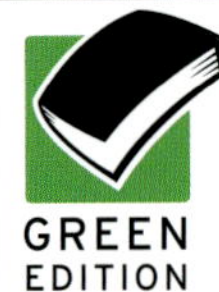

Planet Friendly Publishing
✓ Made in the United States
✓ Printed on Recycled Paper
Text: 10% Cover: 10%
Learn more: www.greenedition.org

At Dover Publications we're committed to producing books in an earth-friendly manner and to helping our customers make greener choices.

Manufacturing books in the United States ensures compliance with strict environmental laws and eliminates the need for international freight shipping, a major contributor to global air pollution.

And printing on recycled paper helps minimize our consumption of trees, water and fossil fuels. The text of *Floral Vector Motifs* was printed on paper made with 10% post-consumer waste, and the cover was printed on paper made with 10% post-consumer waste. According to Environmental Defense's Paper Calculator, by using this innovative paper instead of conventional papers, we achieved the following environmental benefits:

Trees Saved: 4 • Air Emissions Eliminated: 321 pounds
Water Saved: 1,547 gallons • Solid Waste Eliminated: 94 pounds

For more information on our environmental practices, please visit us online at www.doverpublications.com/green

By Alan Weller.
Designed by Joel Waldrep.

Copyright © 2010 by Dover Publications, Inc
Digital images copyright © 2010 by Dover Publications, Inc.
All rights reserved.

Floral Vector Motifs is a new work, first published by Dover Publications, Inc., in 2010.

The illustrations contained in this book and CD-ROM belong to the Dover Vector Motifs Series. They are royalty-free, and may be used as a graphic resource provided no more than ten images are included in the same publication or project. The use of any of these images in book, electronic, or any other format for resale or distribution as royalty-free graphics is strictly prohibited.

For permission to use more than ten images, please contact:
Permissions Department
Dover Publications, Inc.
31 East 2nd Streetw
Mineola, NY 11501
rights@doverpublications.com

The CD-ROM file names correspond to the images in the book. All of the artwork stored on the CD-ROM can be imported directly into a wide range of design and word-processing programs on either Windows or Macintosh platforms. In order to take full advantage of the unique capabilities of the vector format images you will need a vector-editing program such as Adobe Illustrator or CorelDRAW. As a bonus, we have included the freeware vector editor Inkscape on this CD. For more information, see the Read Me! file in the Inkscape folder on the CD. For the most up-to-date information about using the image files on this CD, please visit www.doverpublications.com/991083.

ISBN 10: 0-486-99108-3
ISBN 13: 978-0-486-99108-5

Manufactured in the United States by Courier Corporation
99110501
www.doverpublications.com

001
002
003
004
005

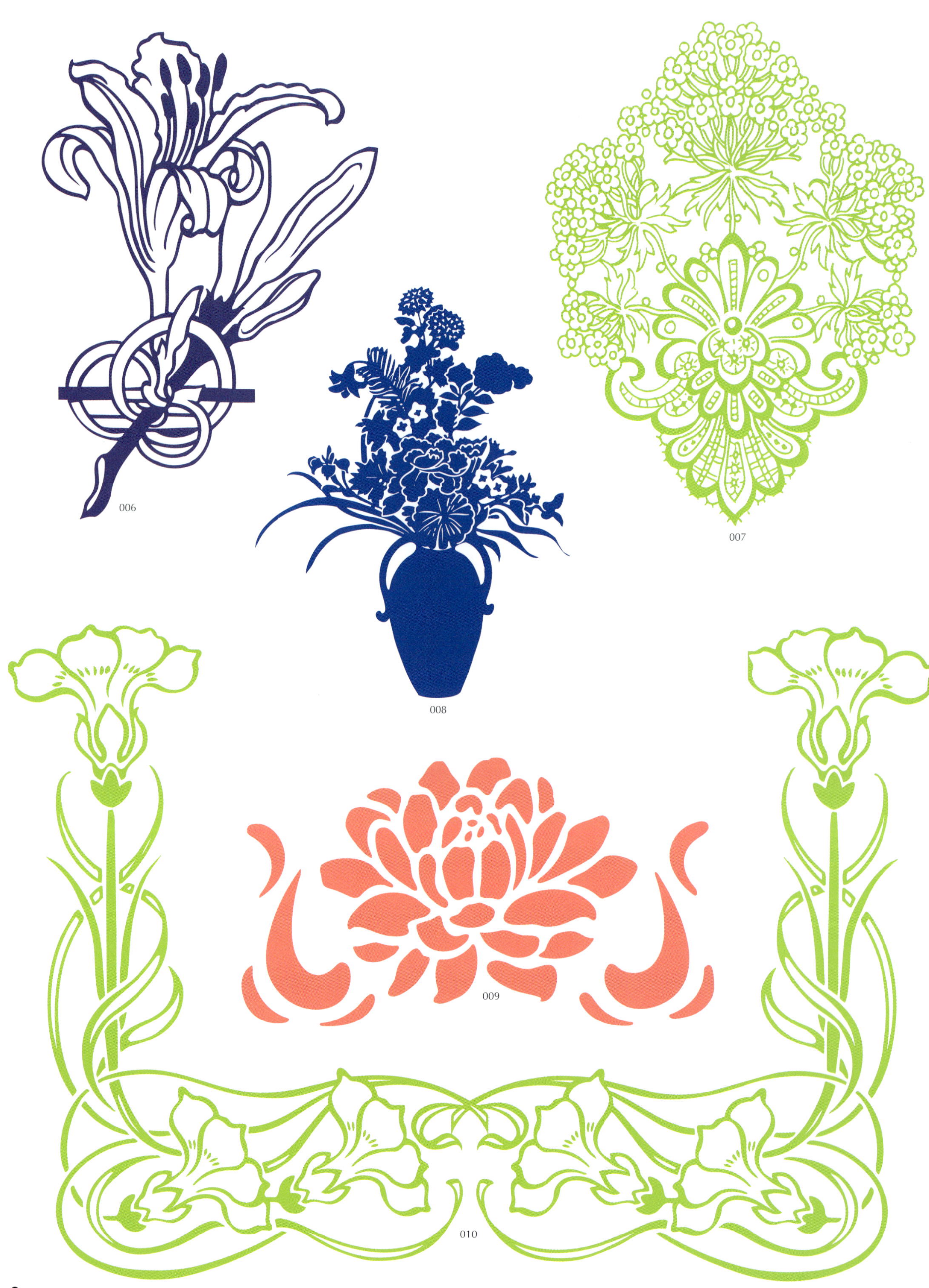
006
007
008
009
010

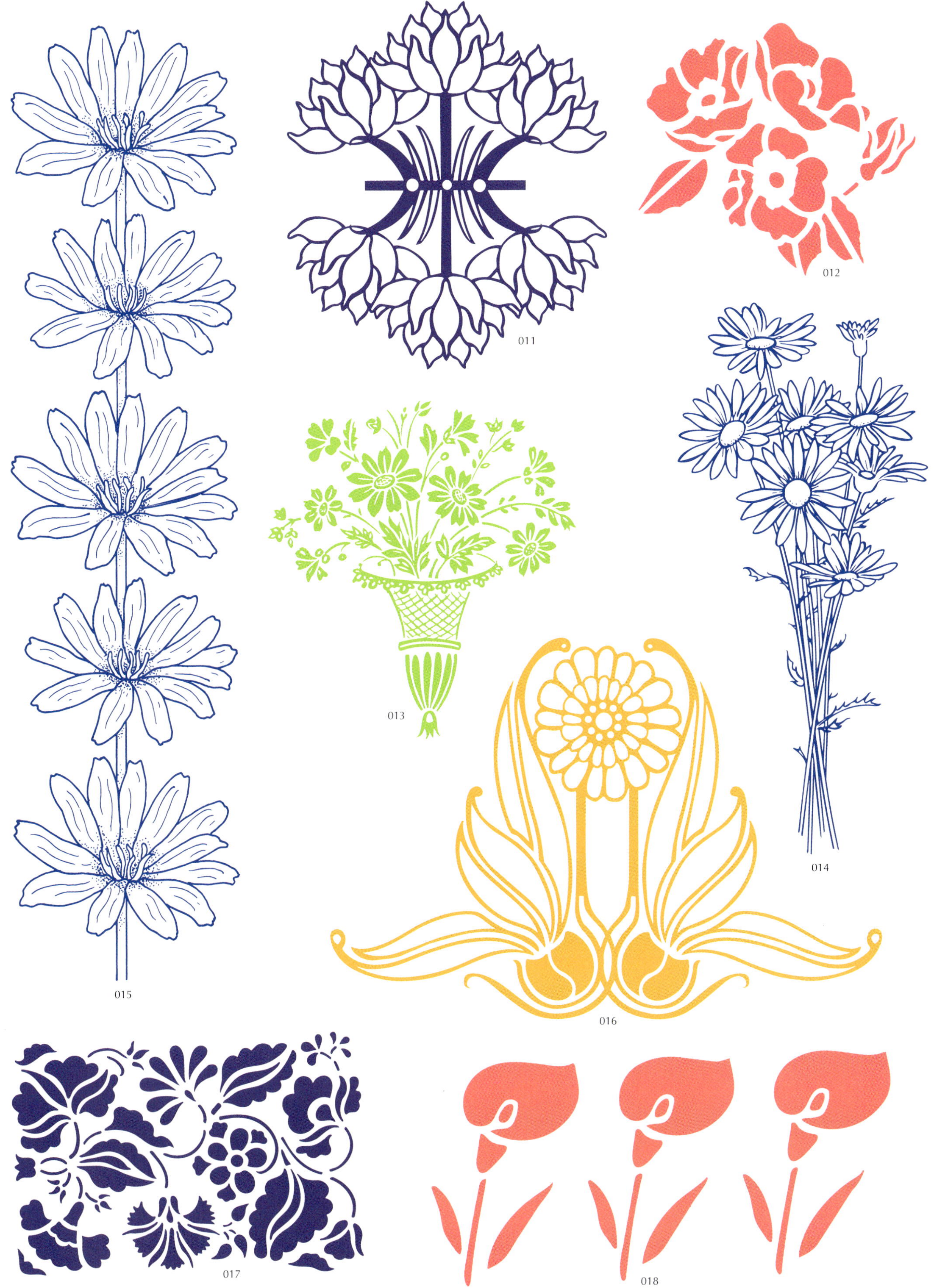

011
012
013
014
015
016
017
018

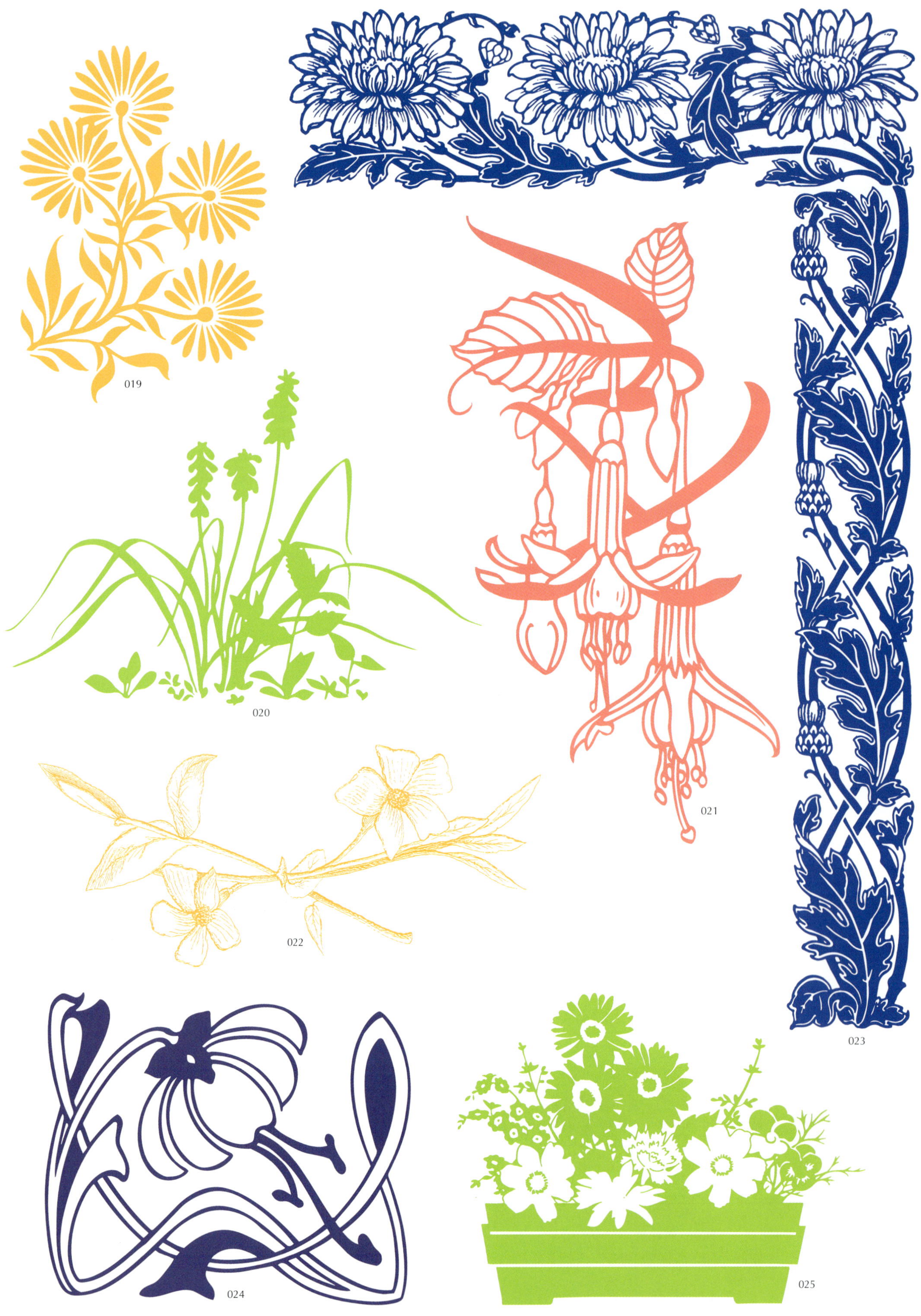

019
020
021
022
023
024
025

026
027
028
029
030
031
032

033
034
035
036
037
038
039

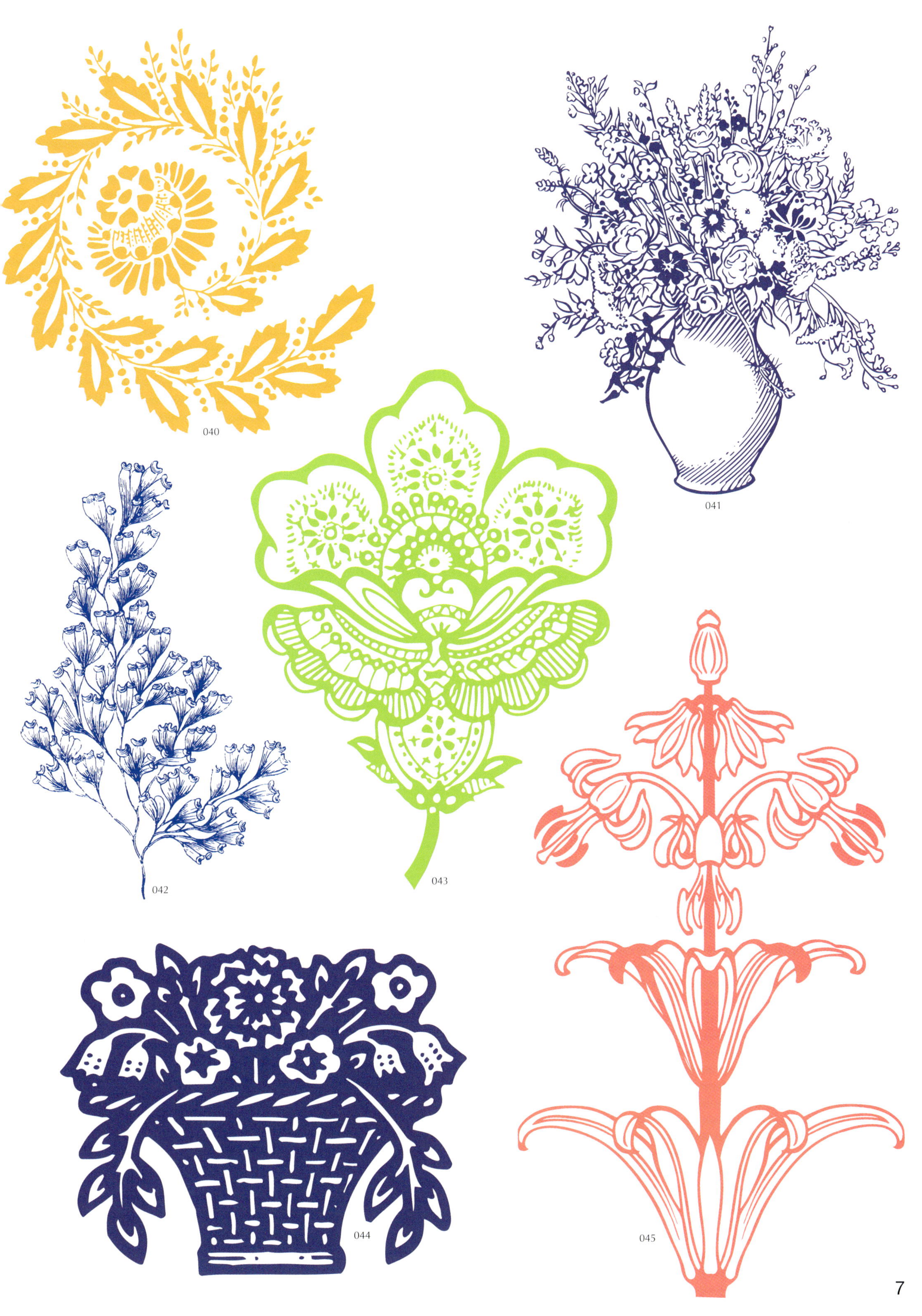
040
041
042
043
044
045

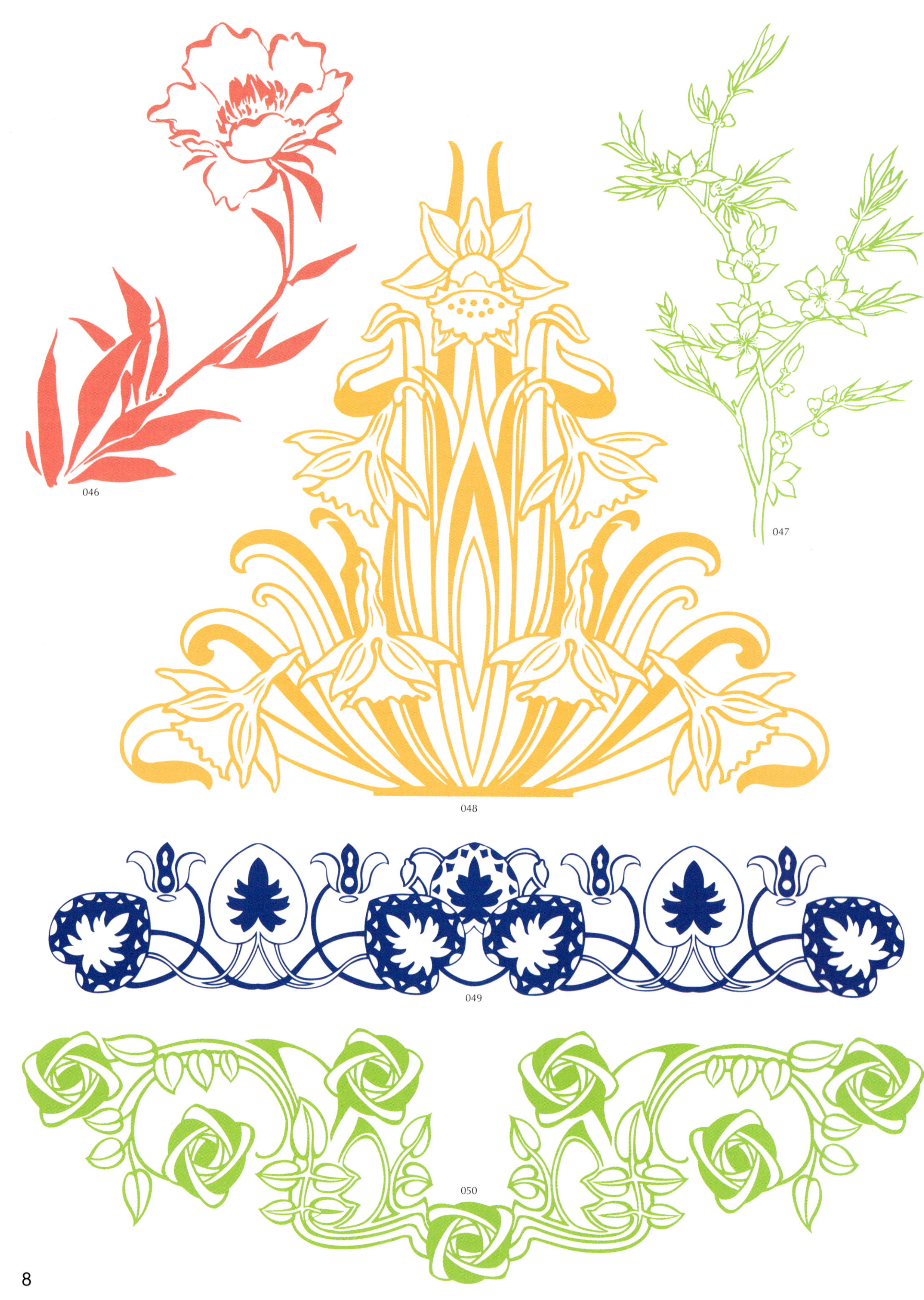

046

047

048

049

050

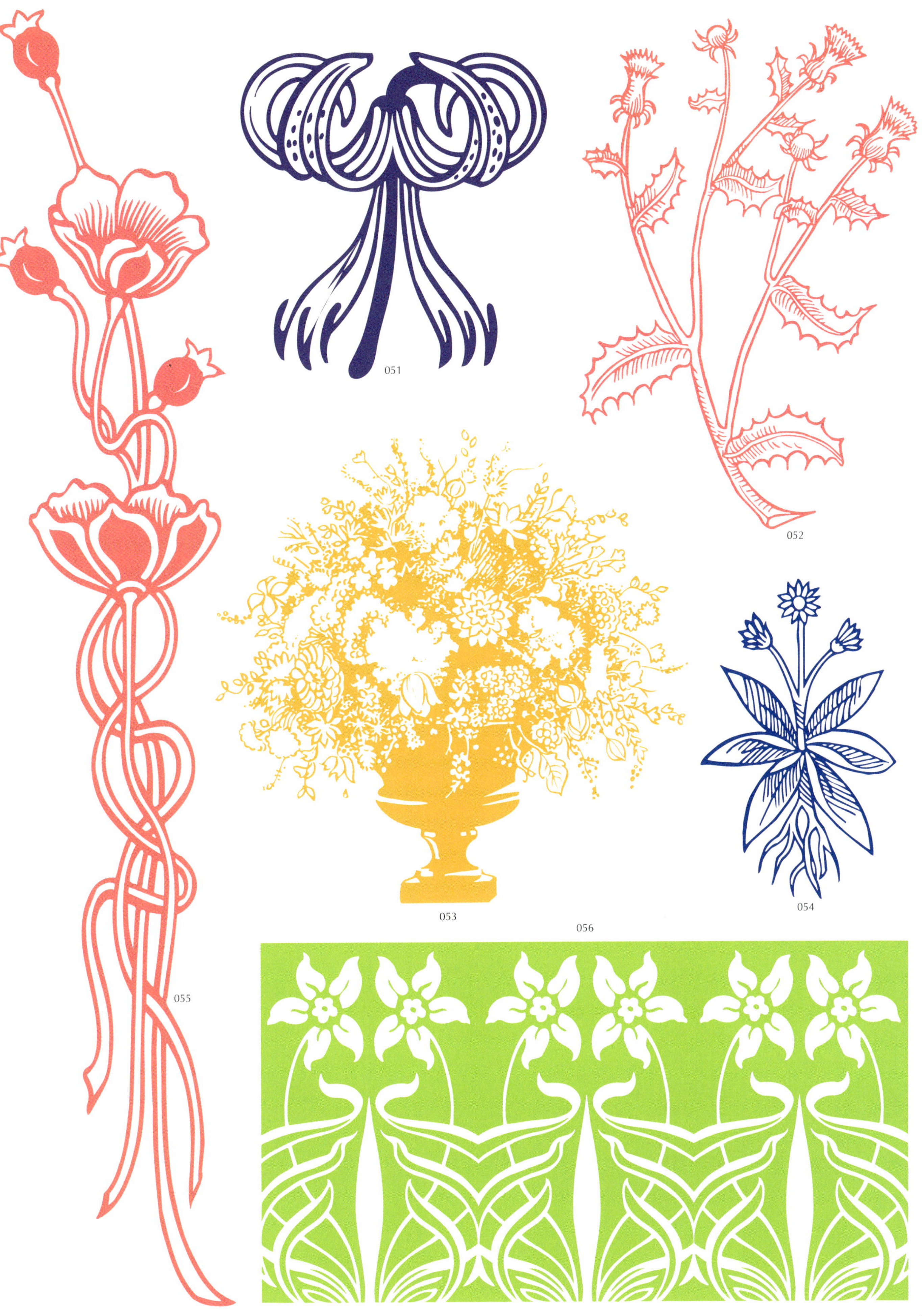

051

052

053

054

056

055

057
058
059
060
061
062
063
064

065
066
067
068
069
070

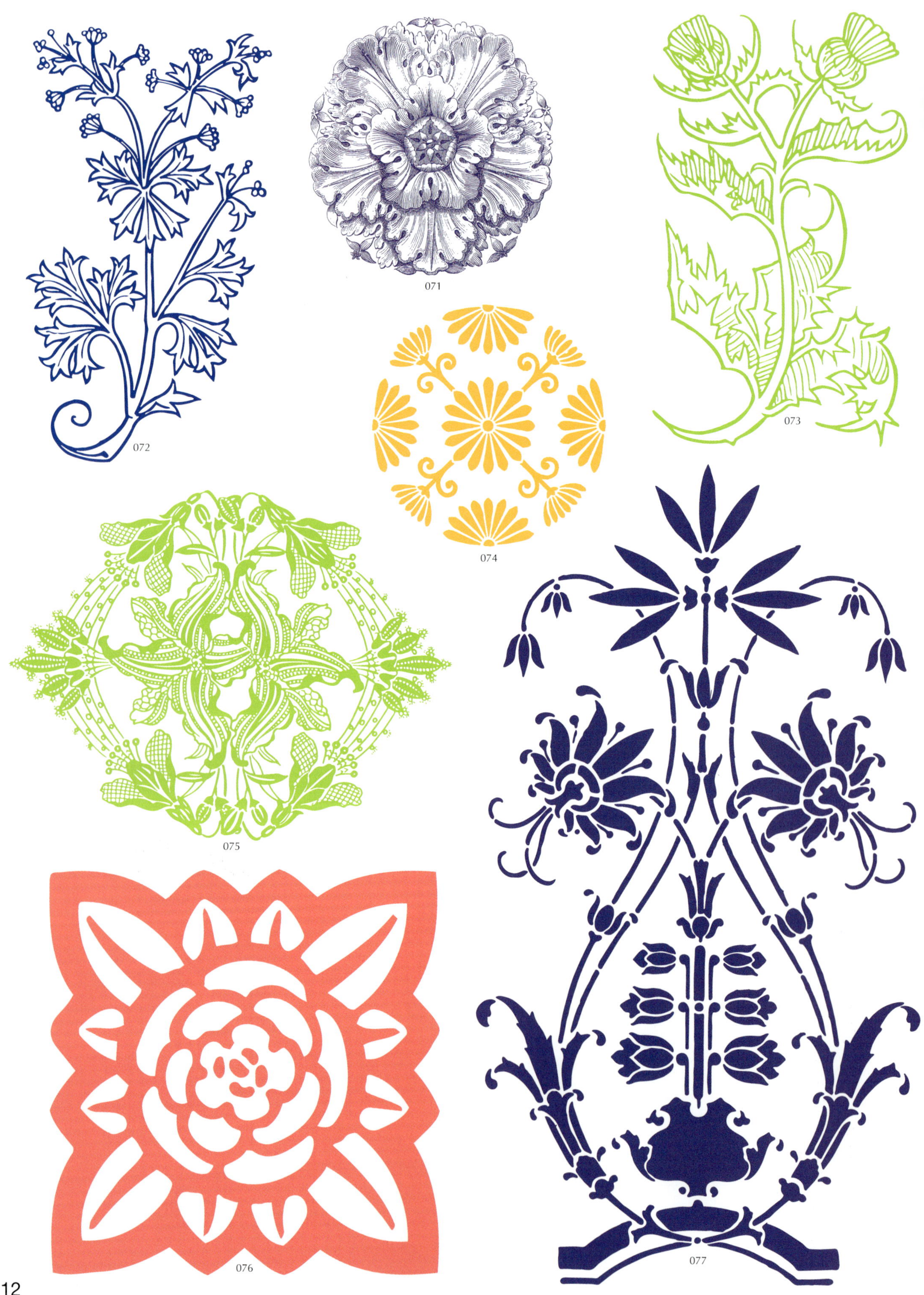

071
072
073
074
075
076
077

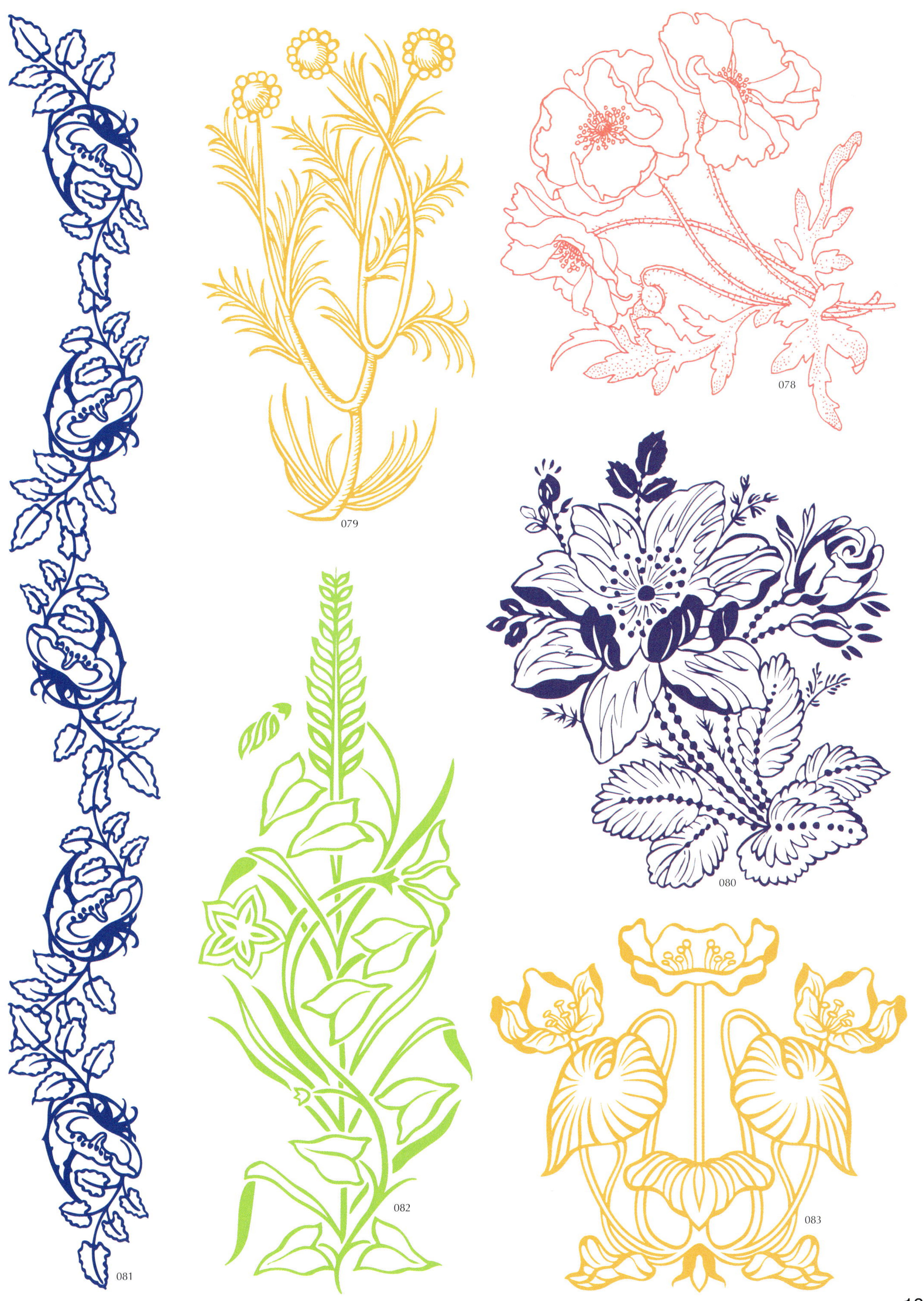
079
078
080
081
082
083

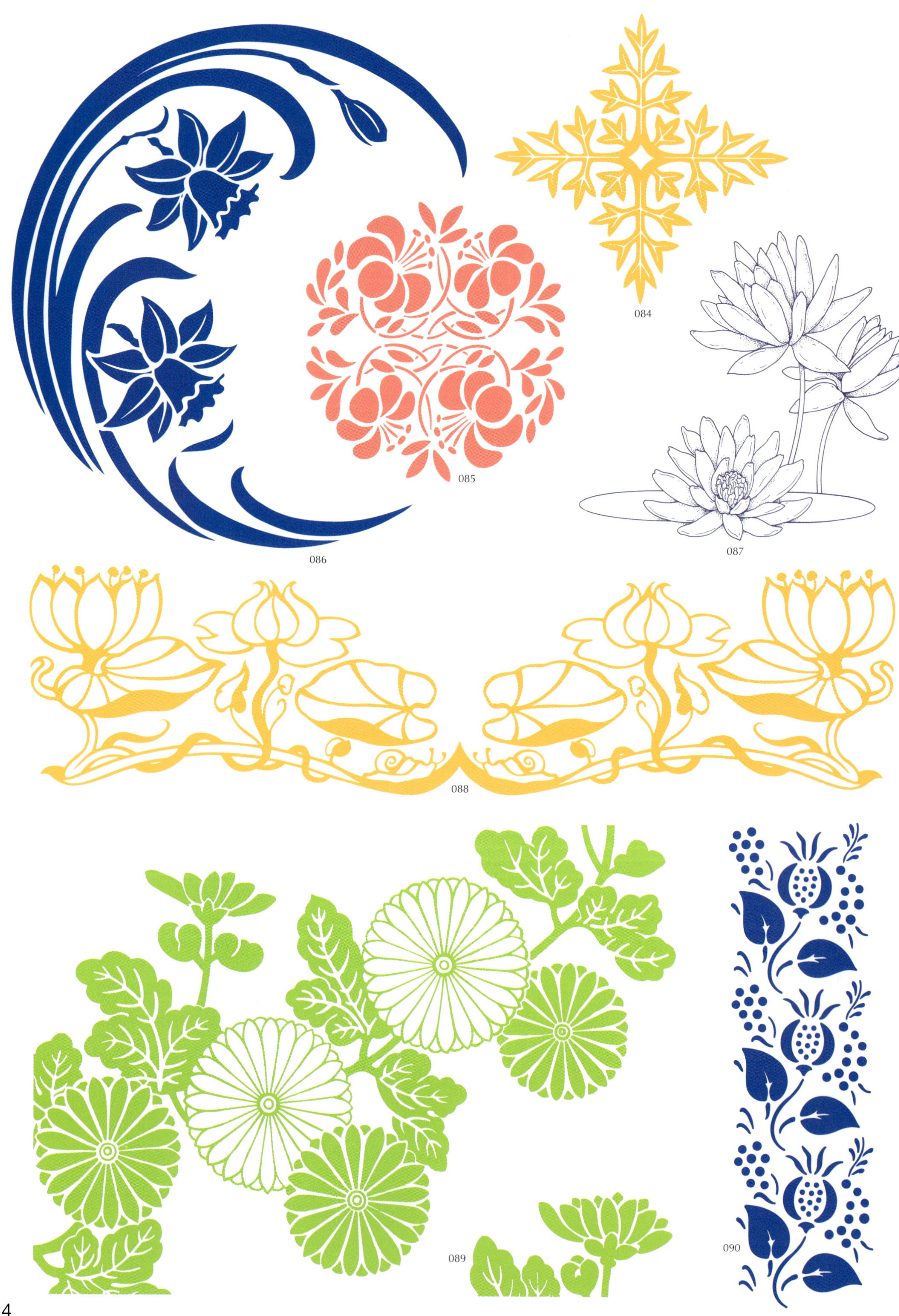
084
085
086
087
088
089
090

091

092

093

094

095

096

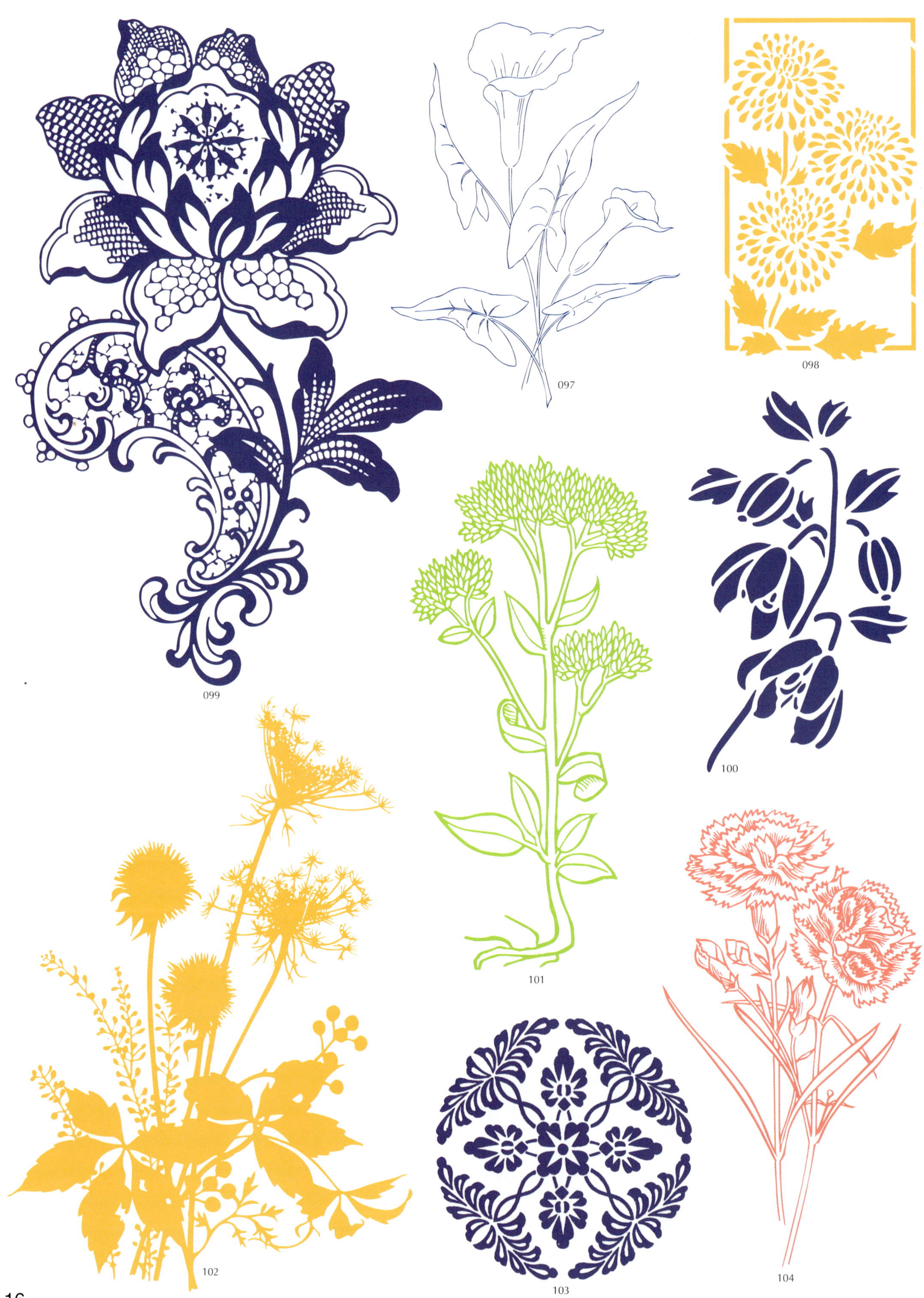
097
098
099
100
101
102
103
104

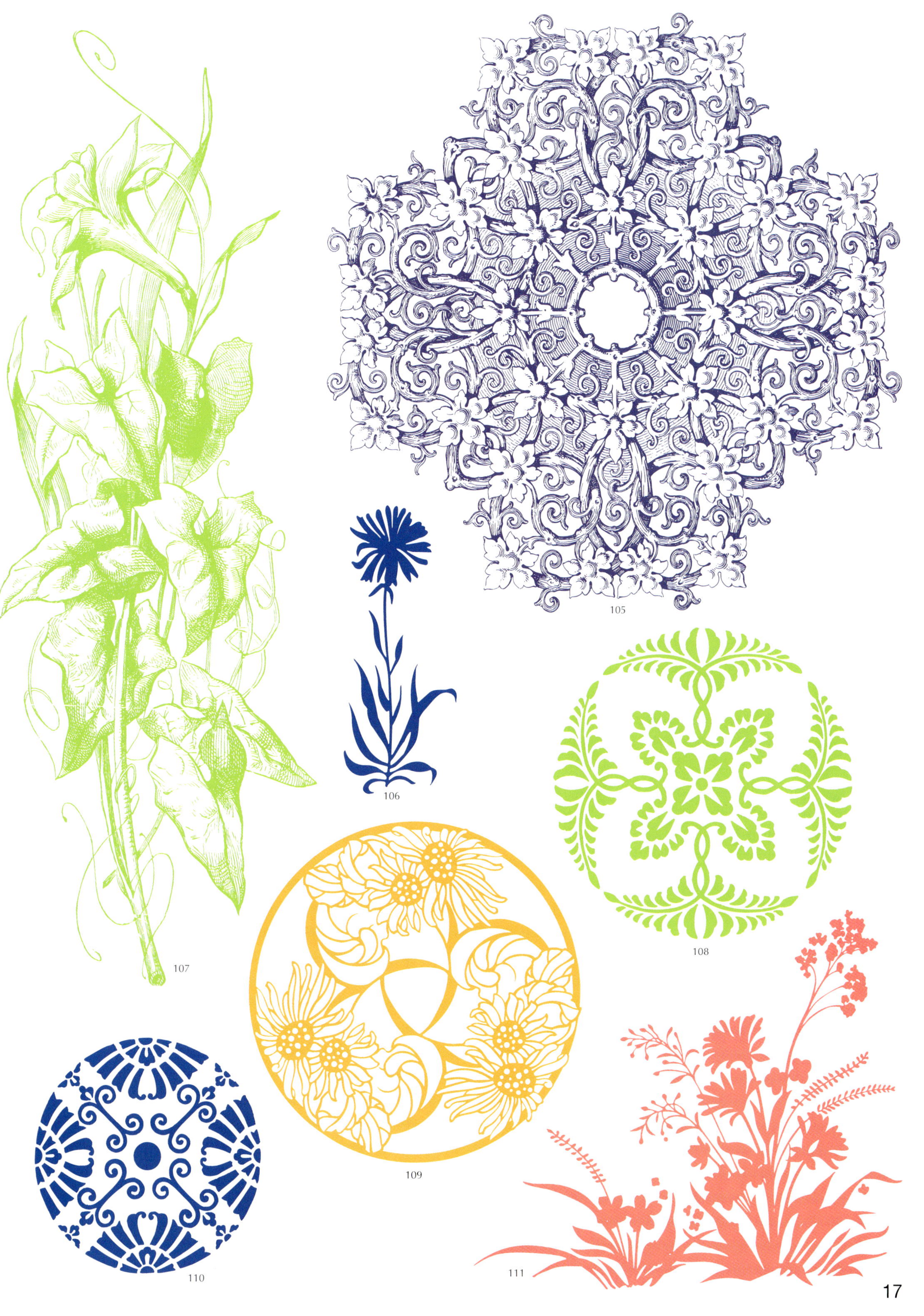

105
106
107
108
109
110
111

112
113
114
115
116
117

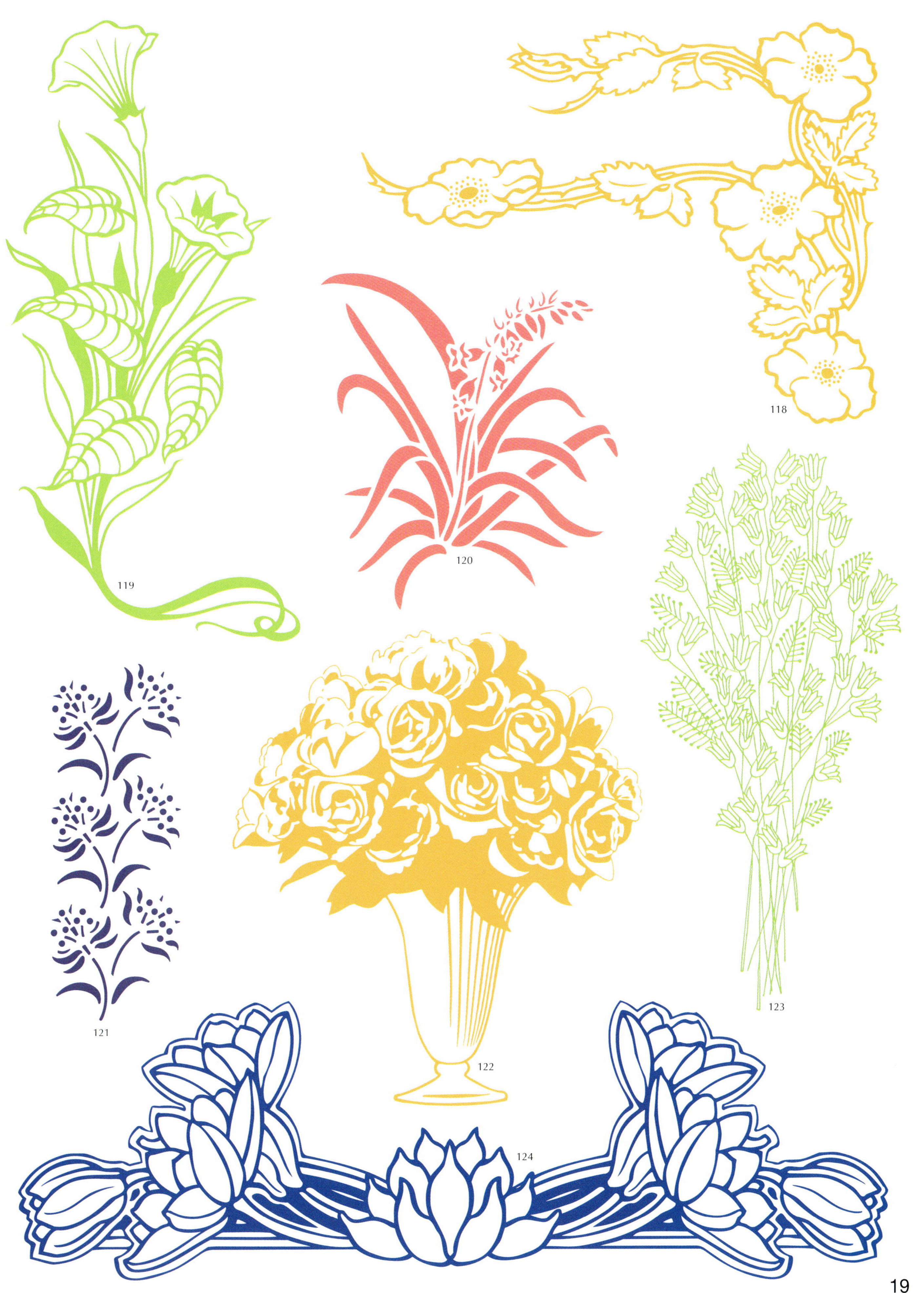
118
119
120
123
121
122
124

125 126 127 128 129 130

131
132
133
134
135
136
137

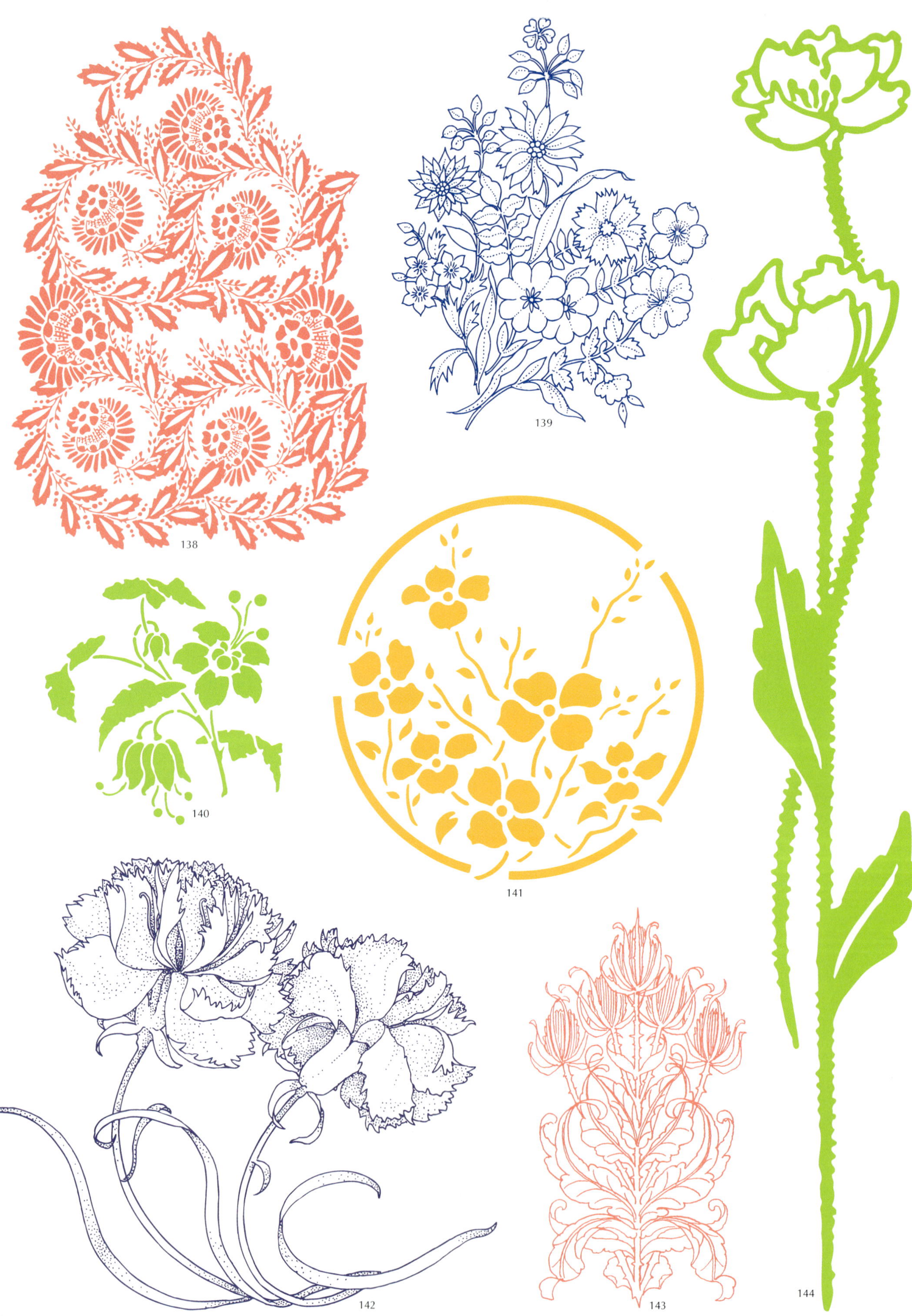
138
139
140
141
142
143
144

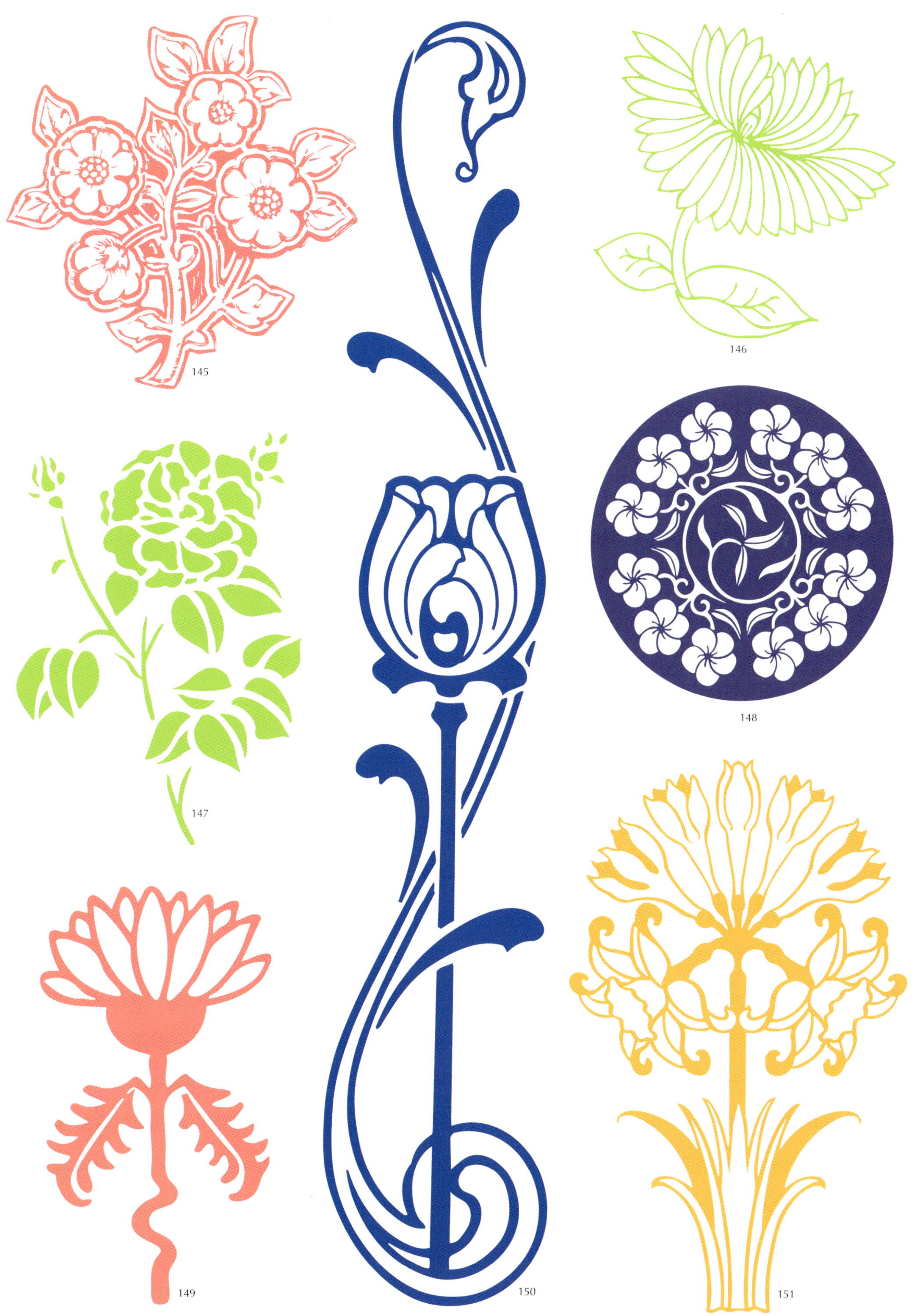

145
146
147
148
149
150
151

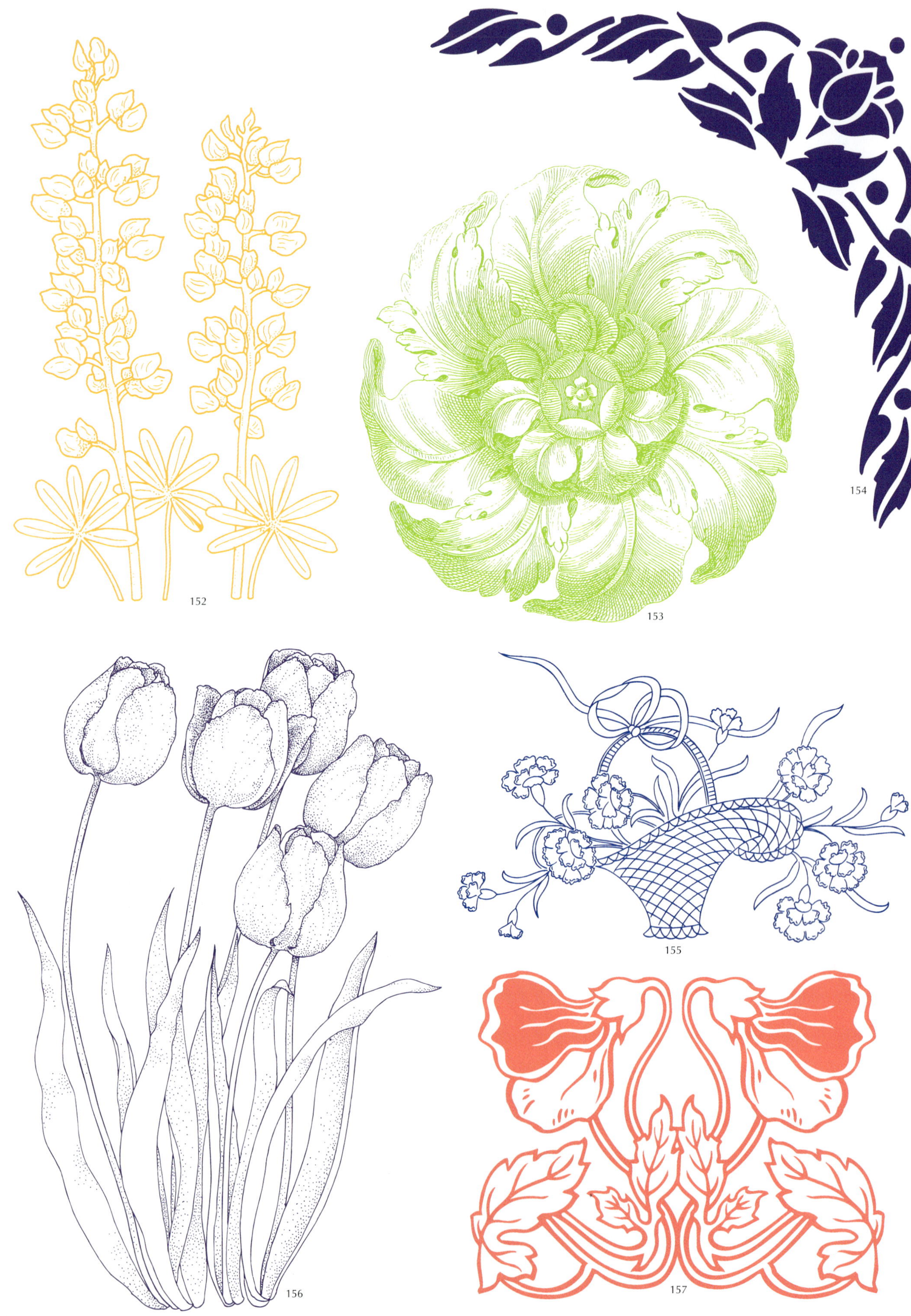
152
153
154
155
156
157

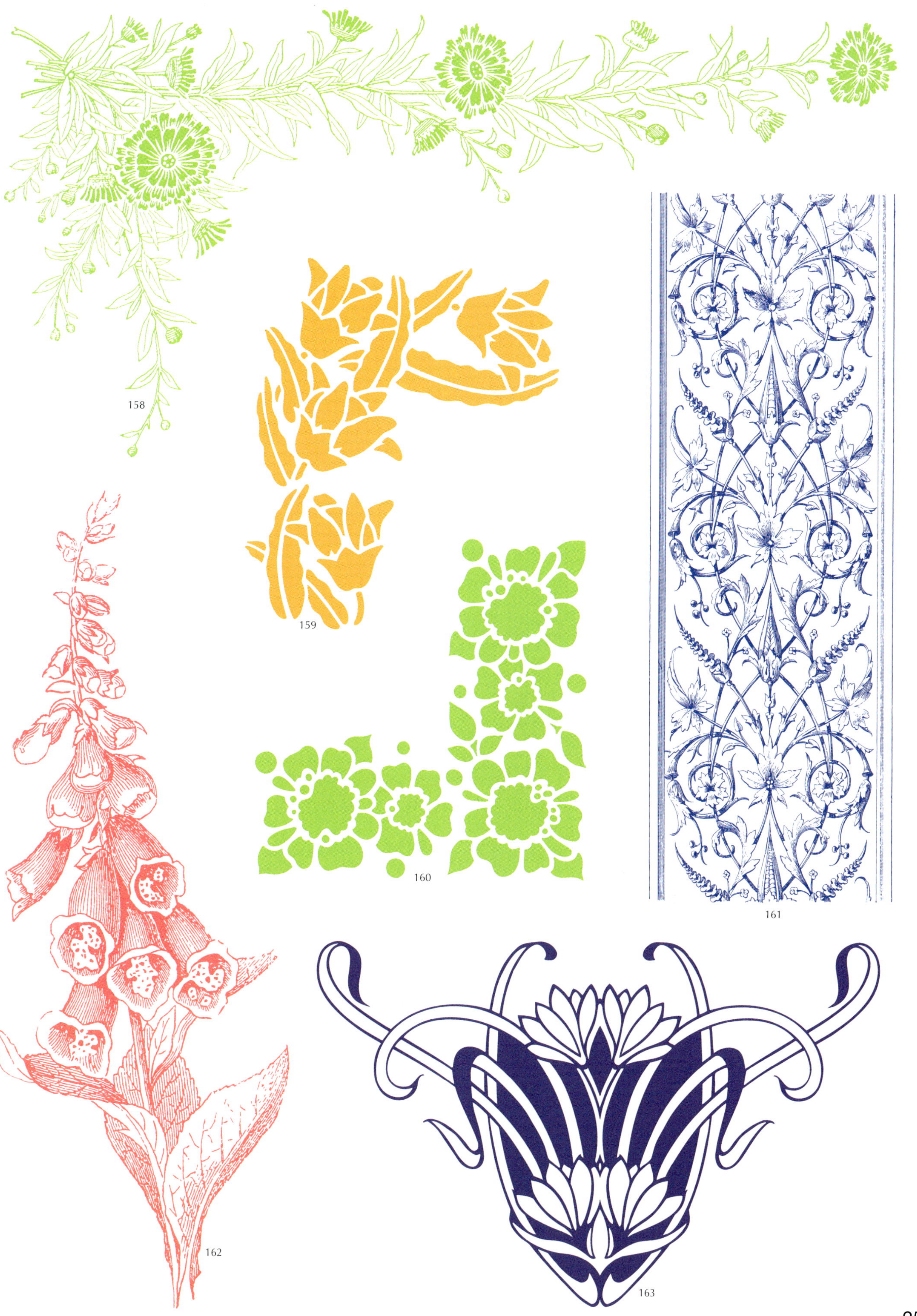

158

159

160

161

162

163

164

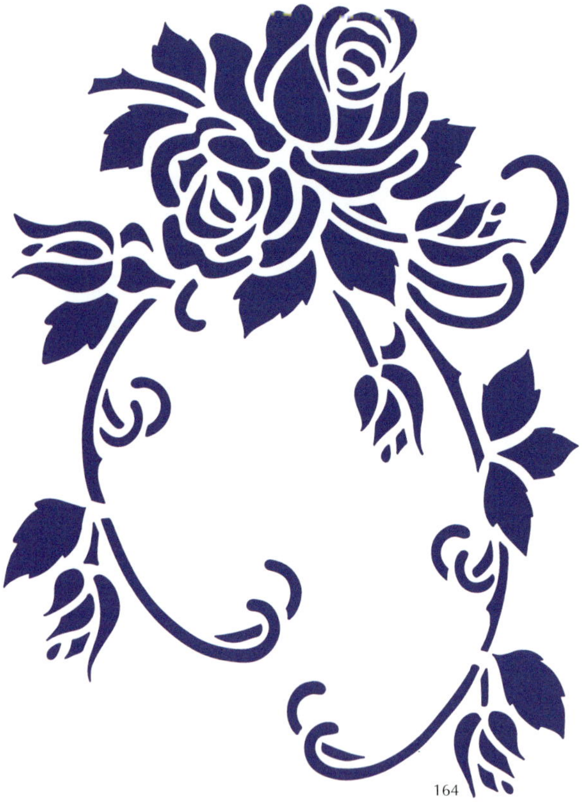

165

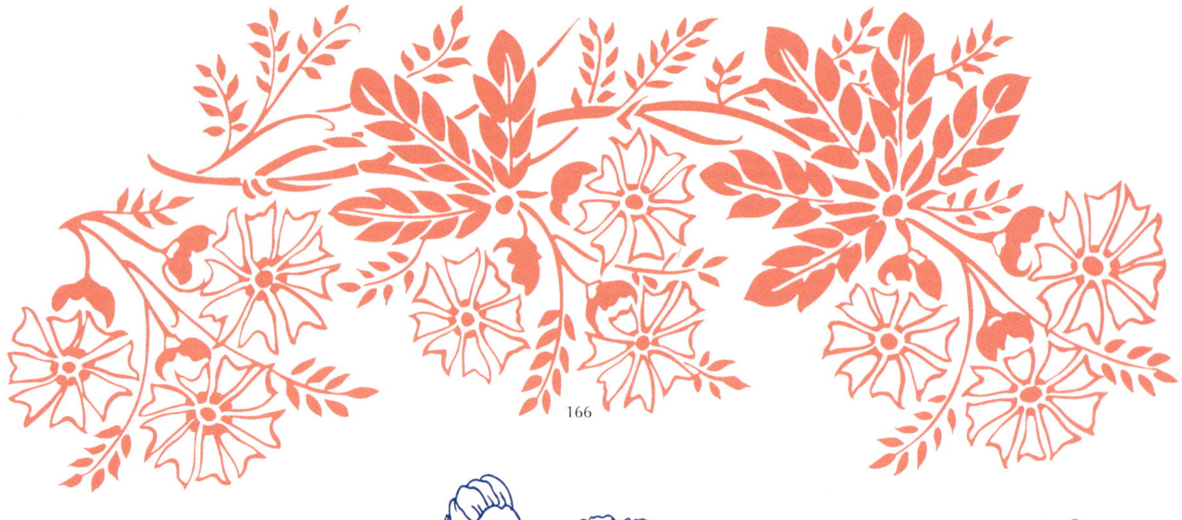

166

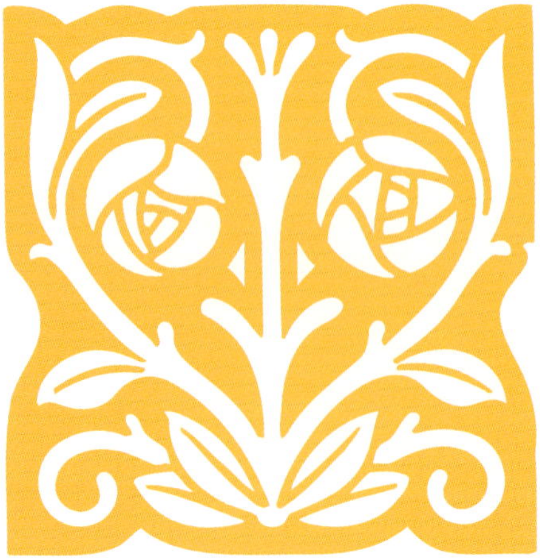

167

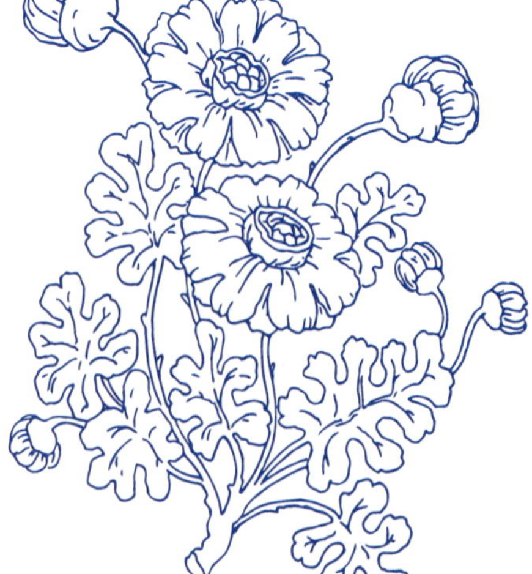

168

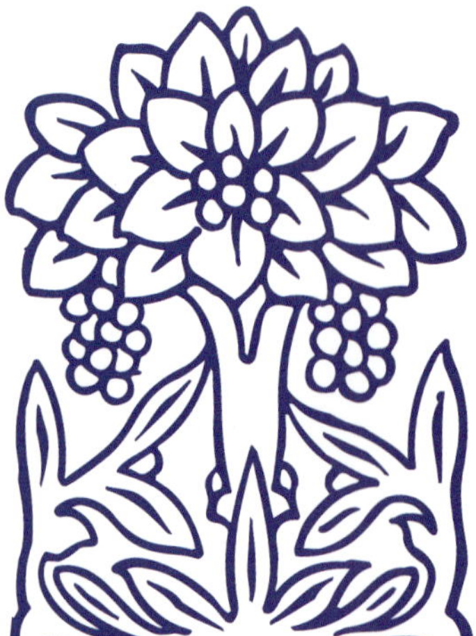

169

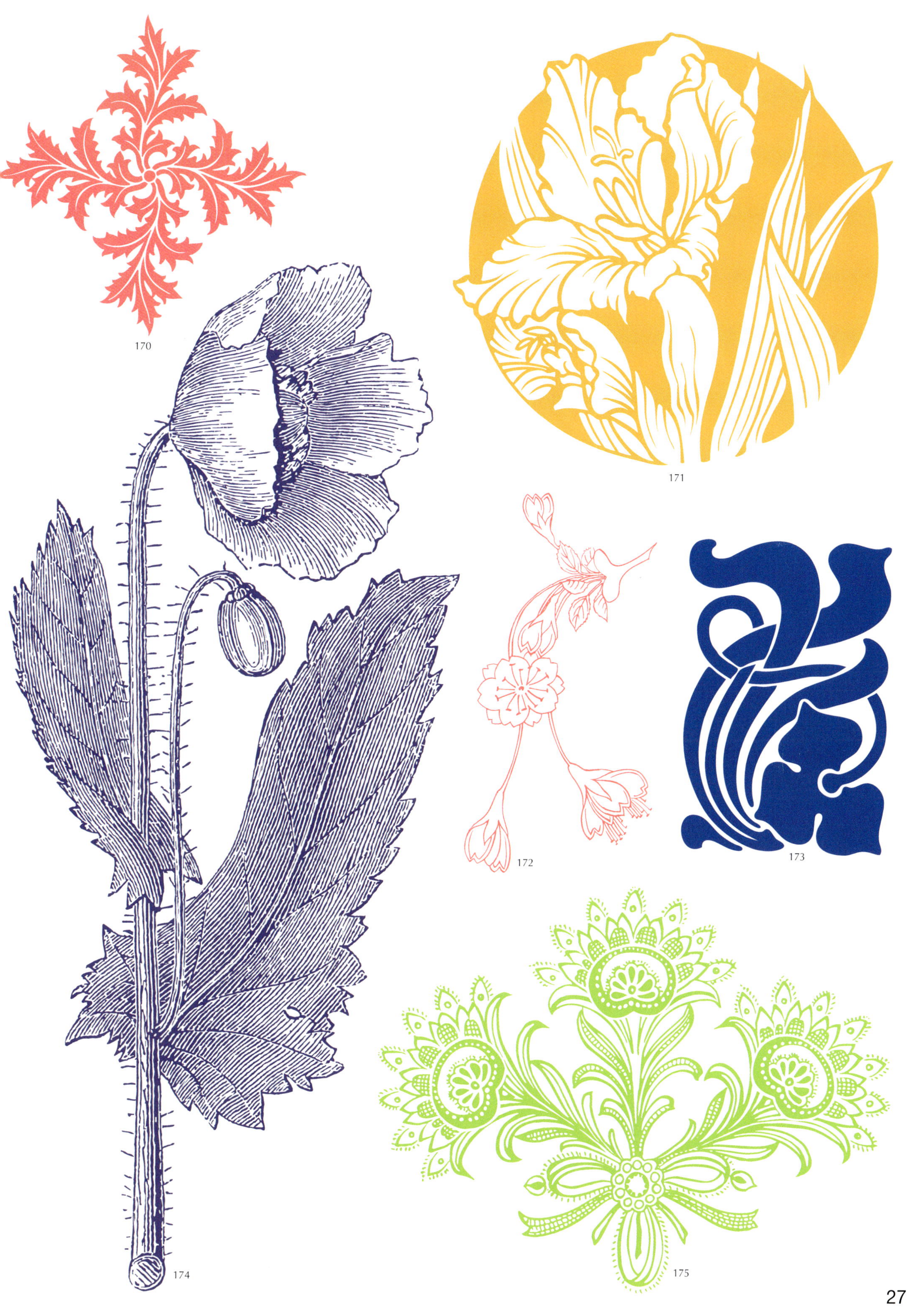

170

171

172

173

174

175

177
176
178
179
180

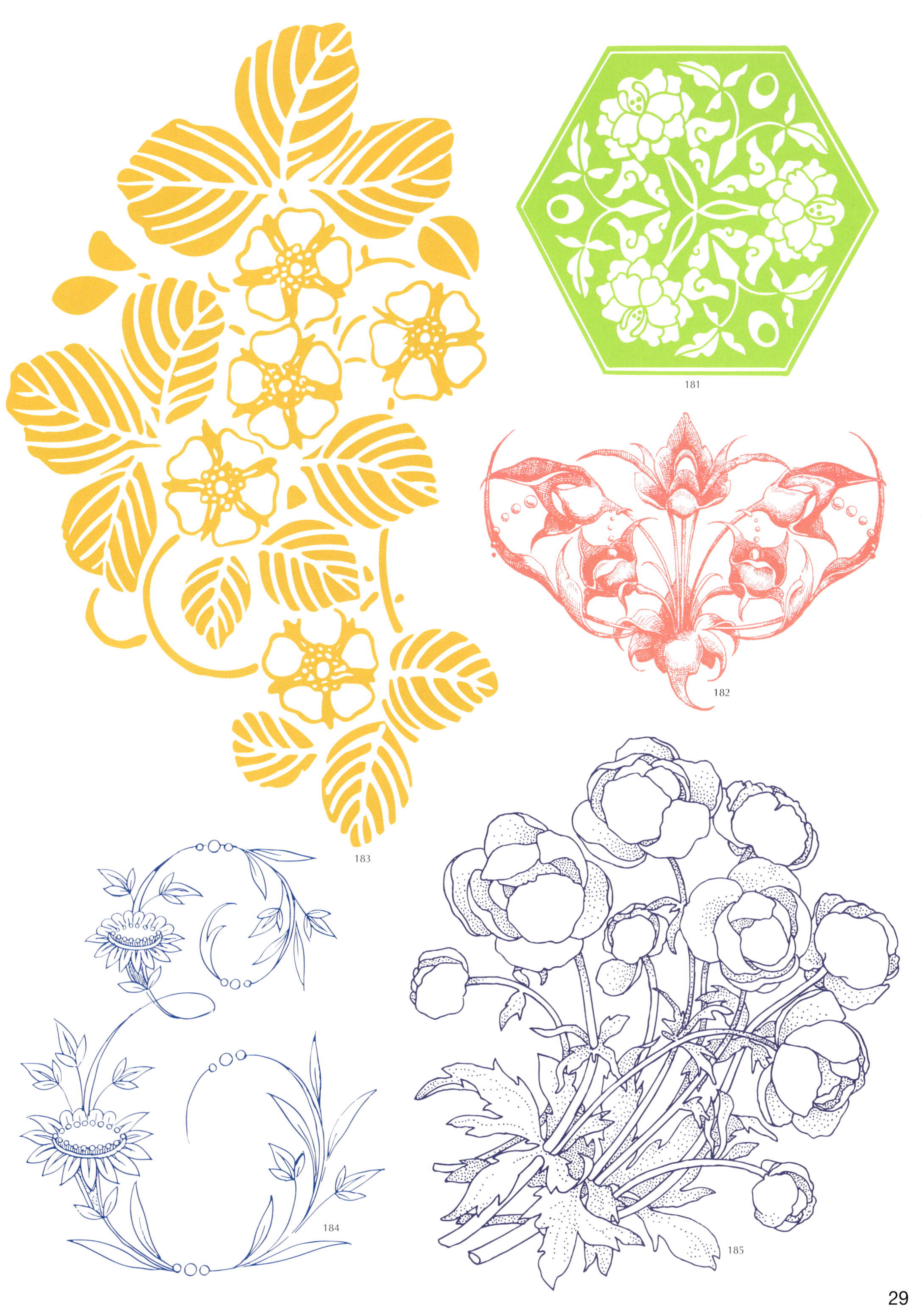
181
182
183
184
185

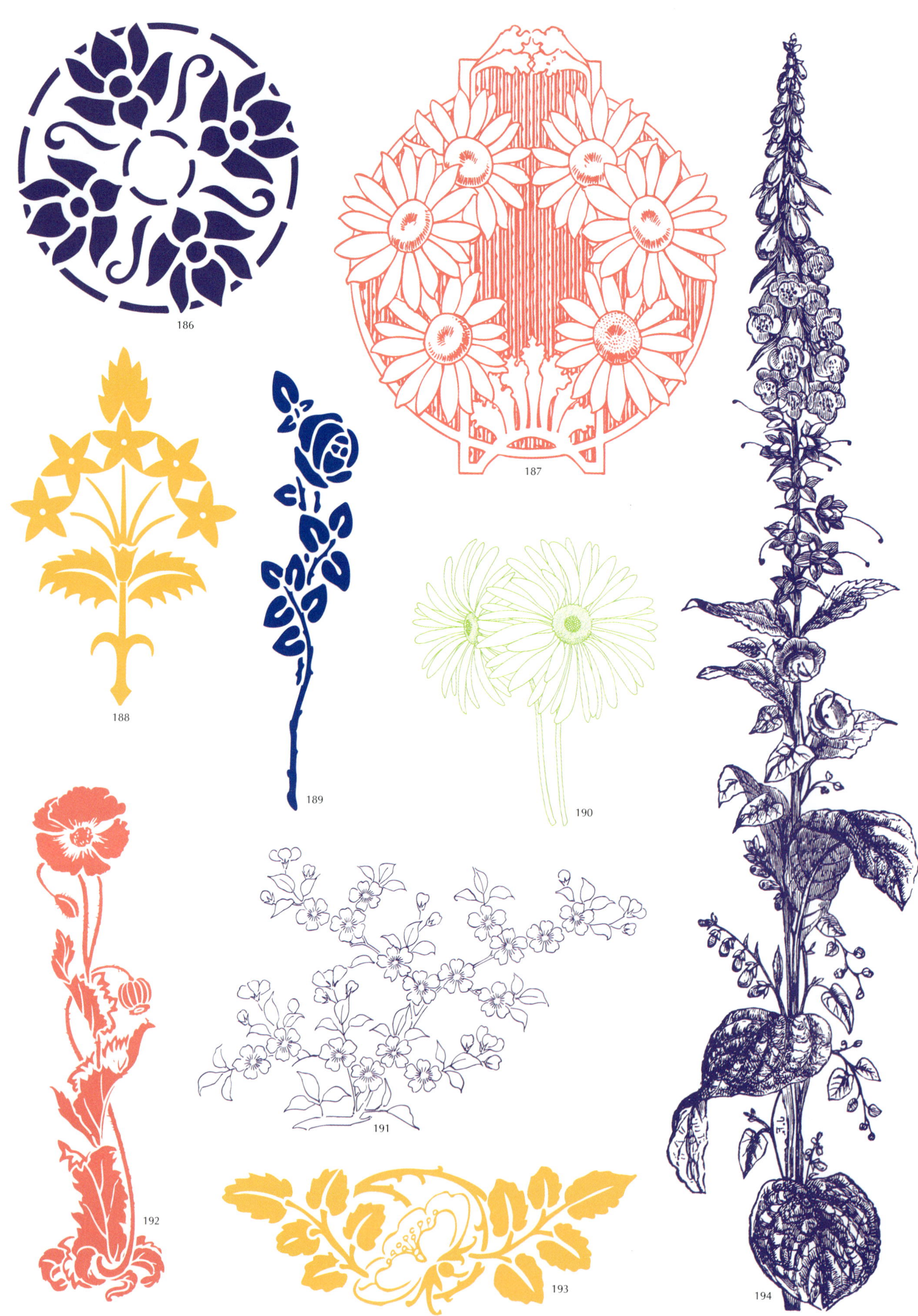
186
187
188
189
190
191
192
193
194

195
196
197
198
199
200
201
202

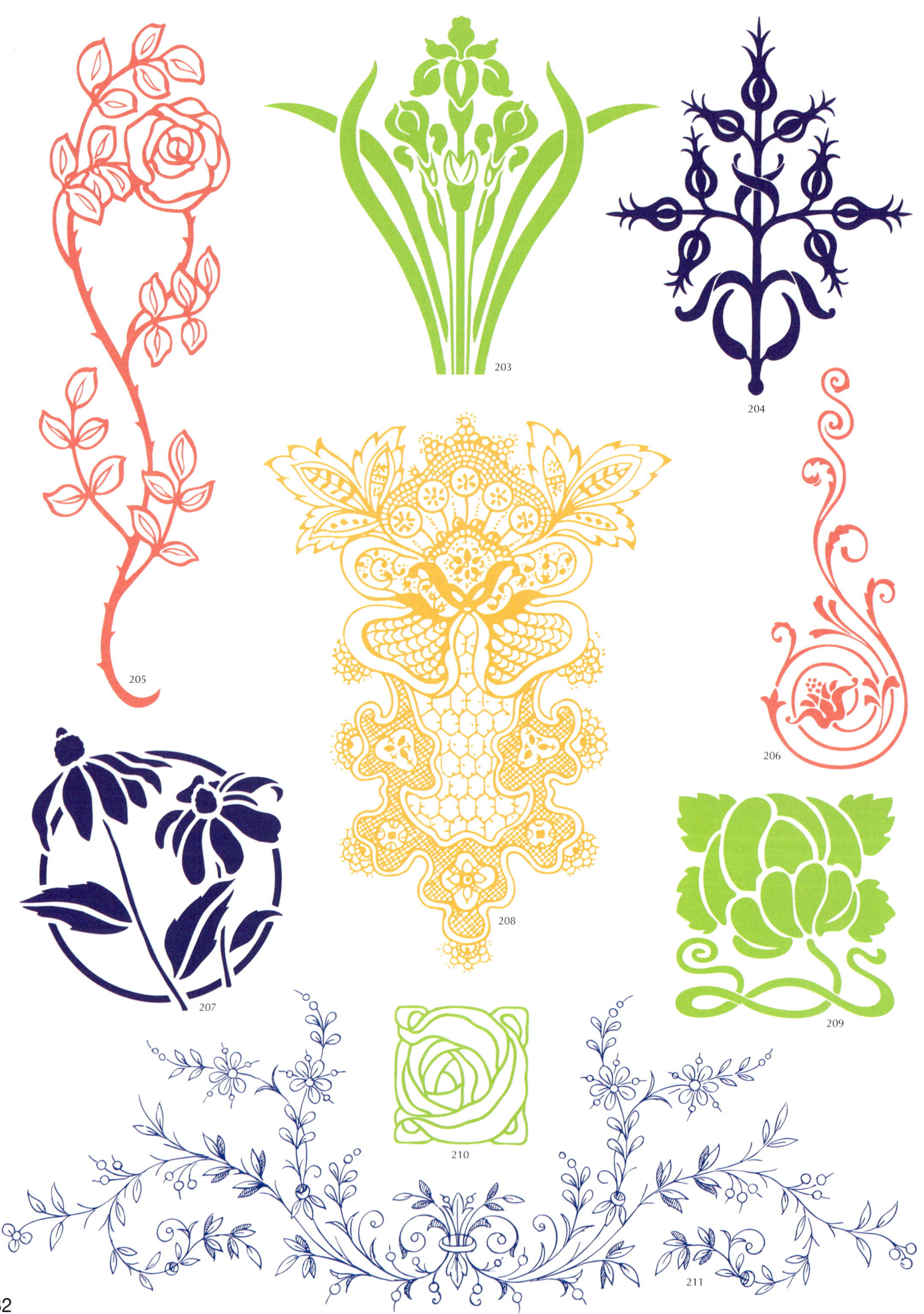
203
204
205
206
207
208
209
210
211

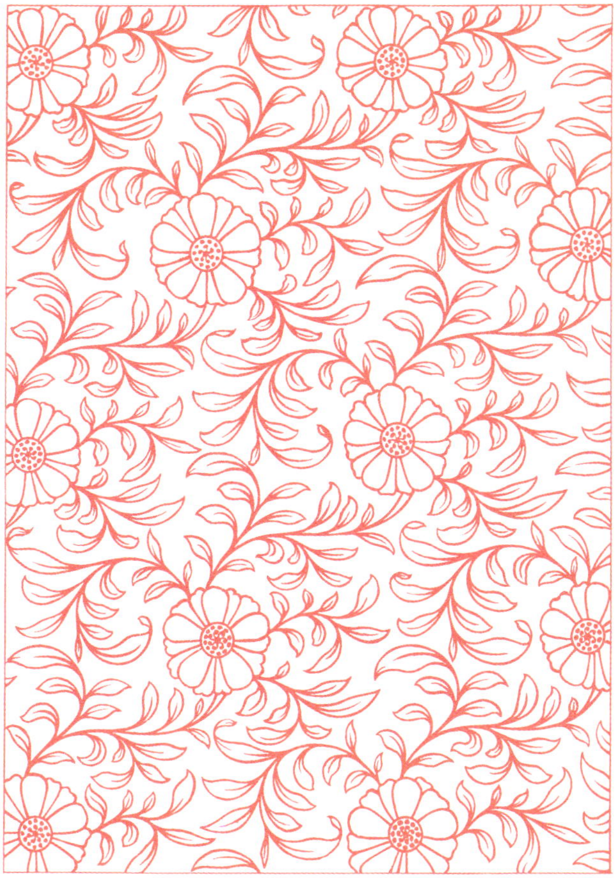

212

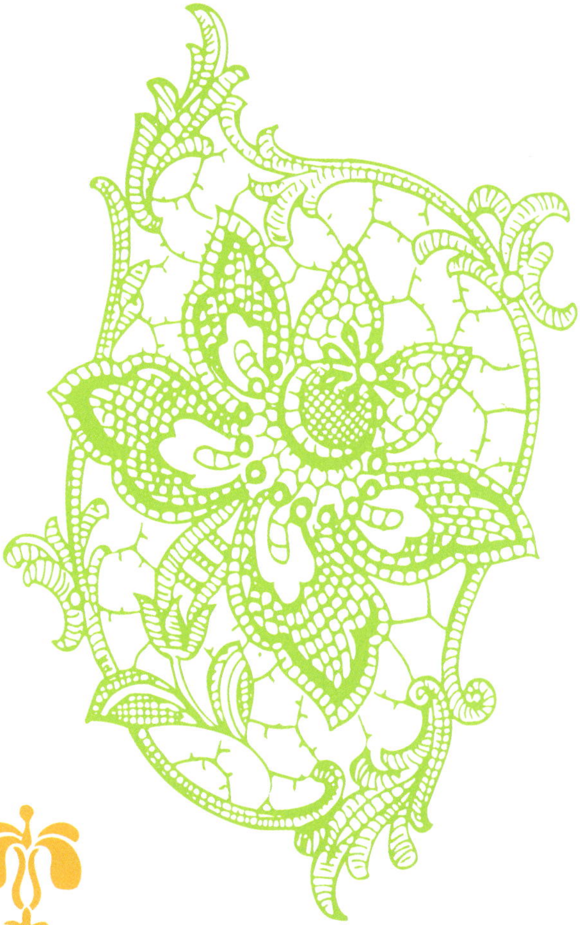

213

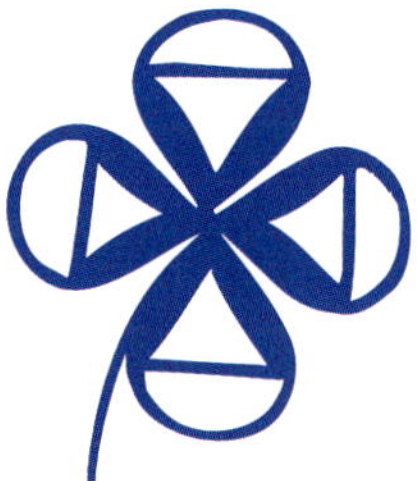

214

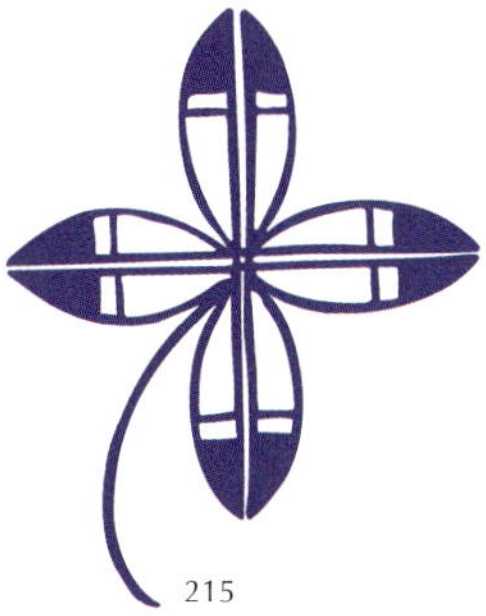

215

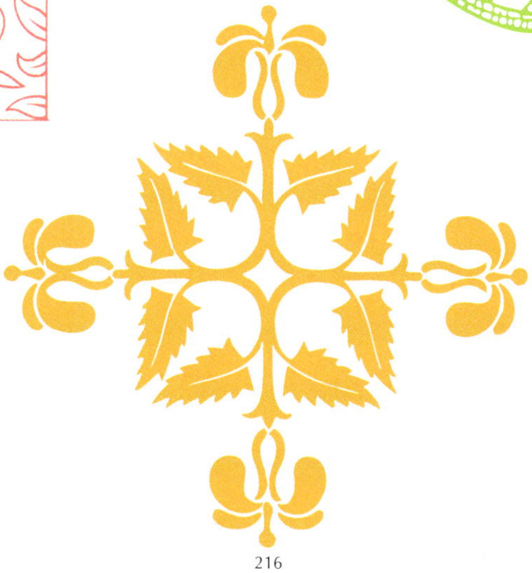

216

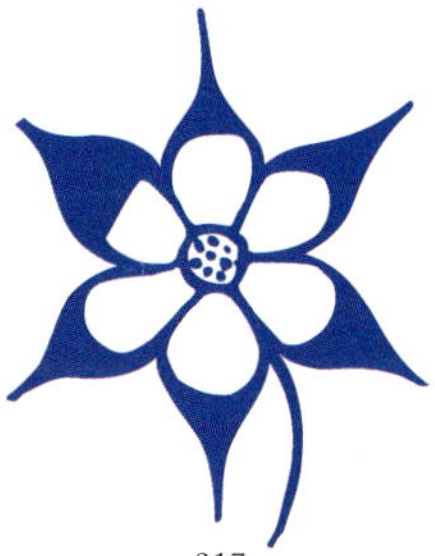

217

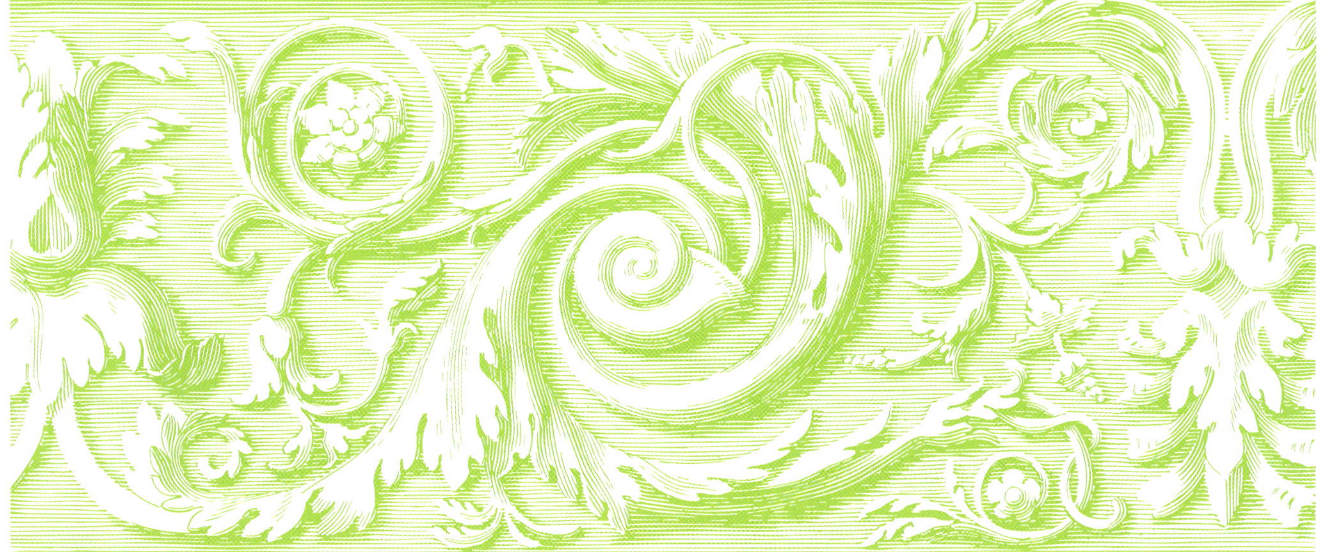

218

219
220
221
222
223
224
225

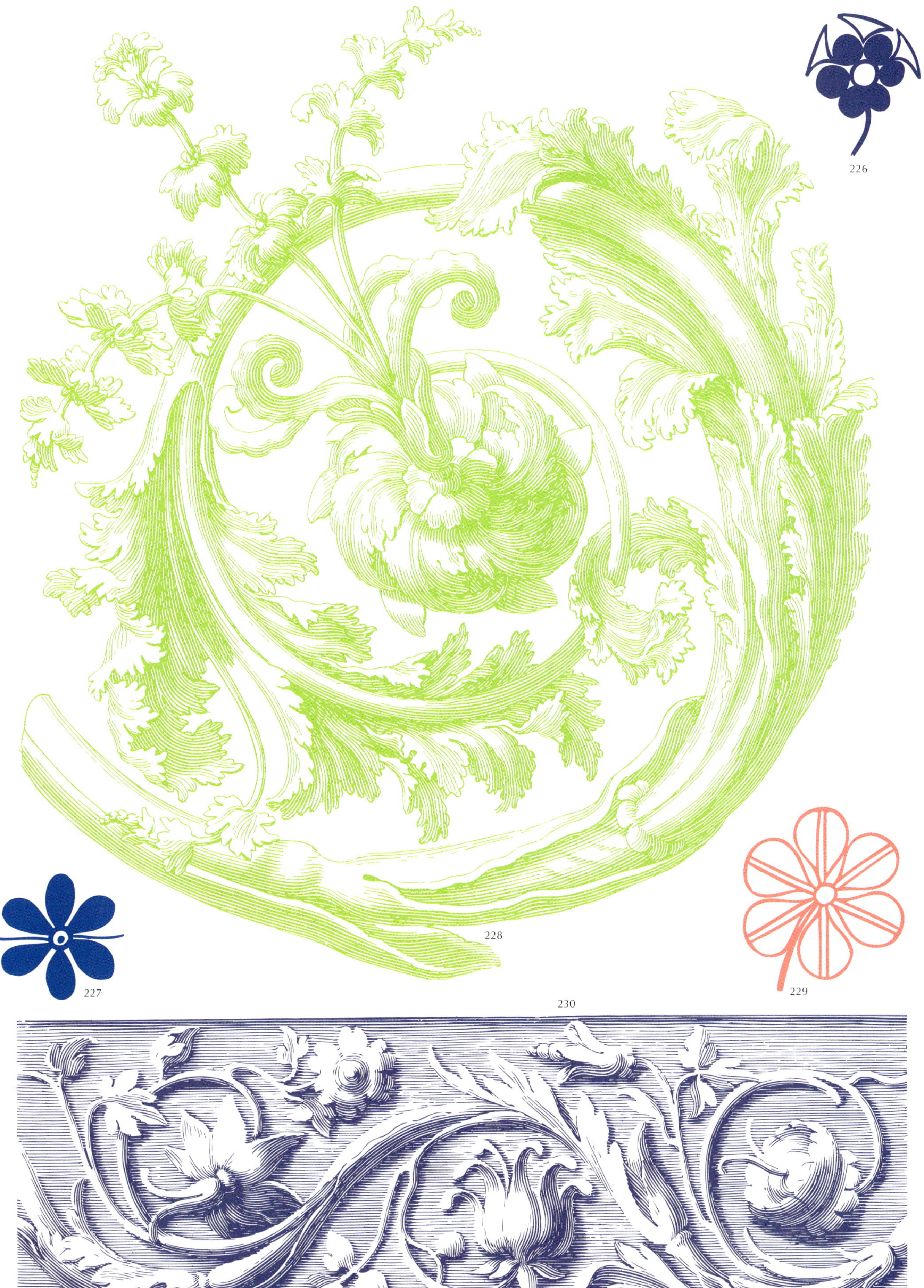

226

228

227

229

230

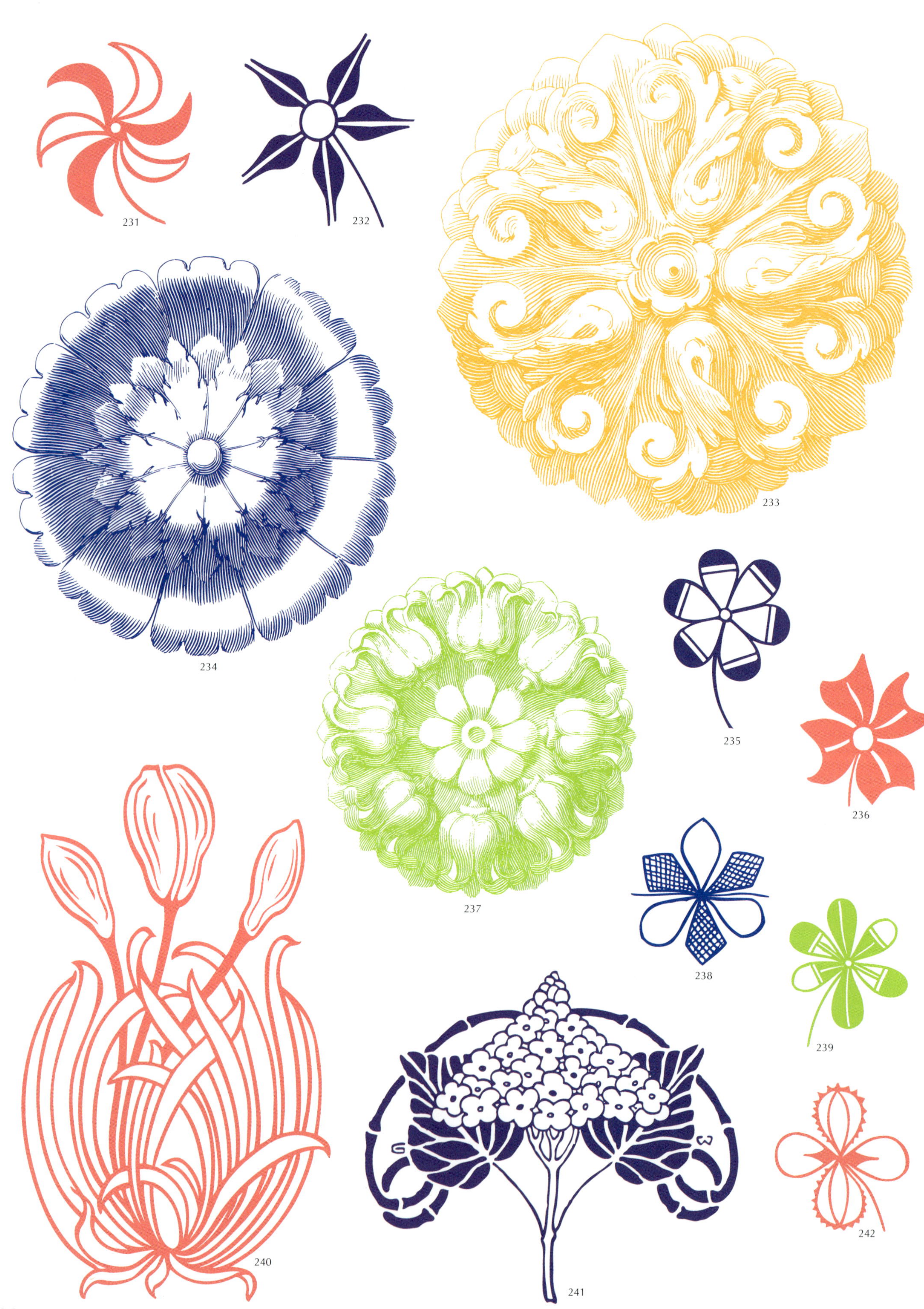
231
232
233
234
235
236
237
238
239
240
241
242

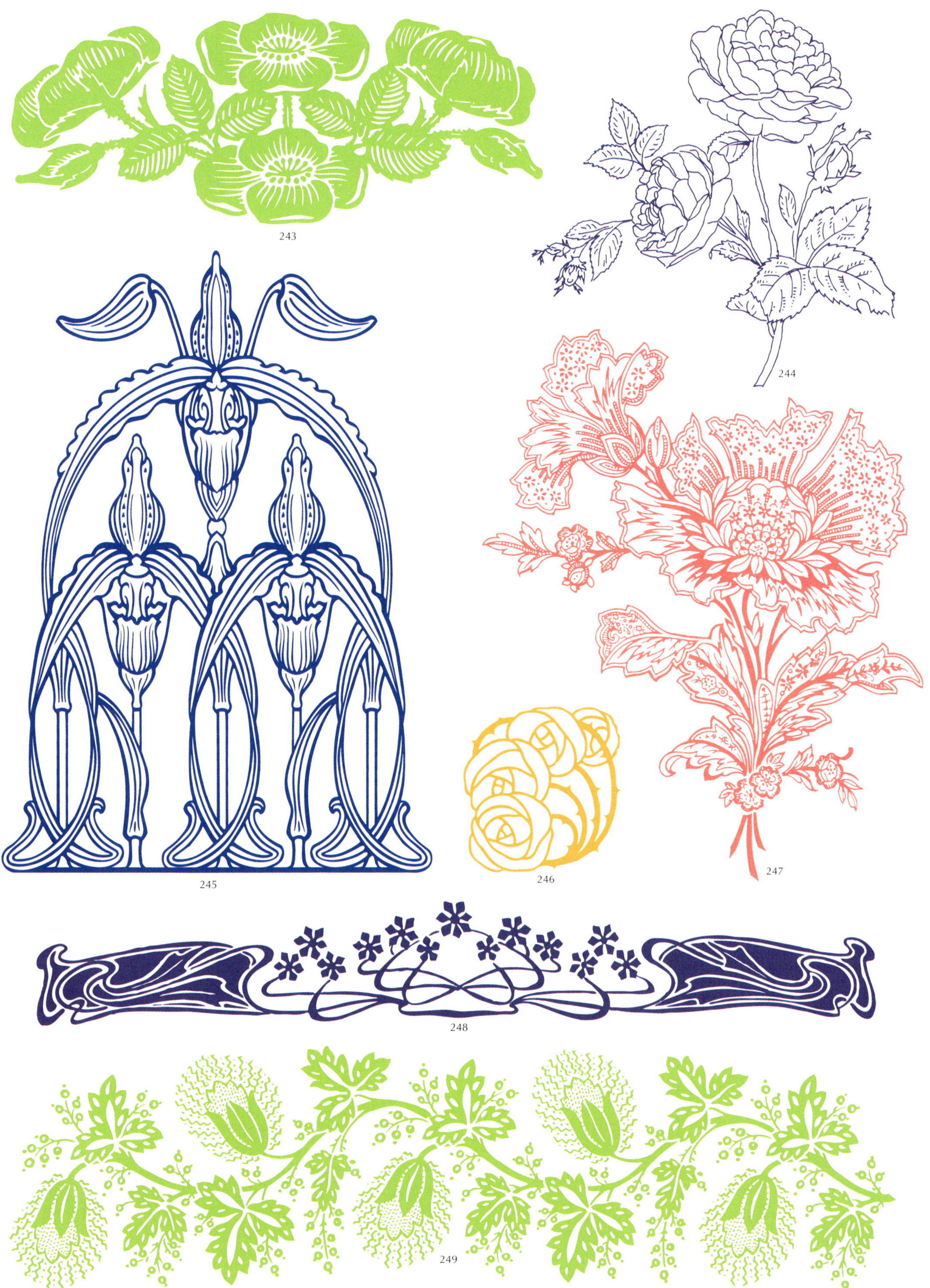
243
244
245
246
247
248
249

250

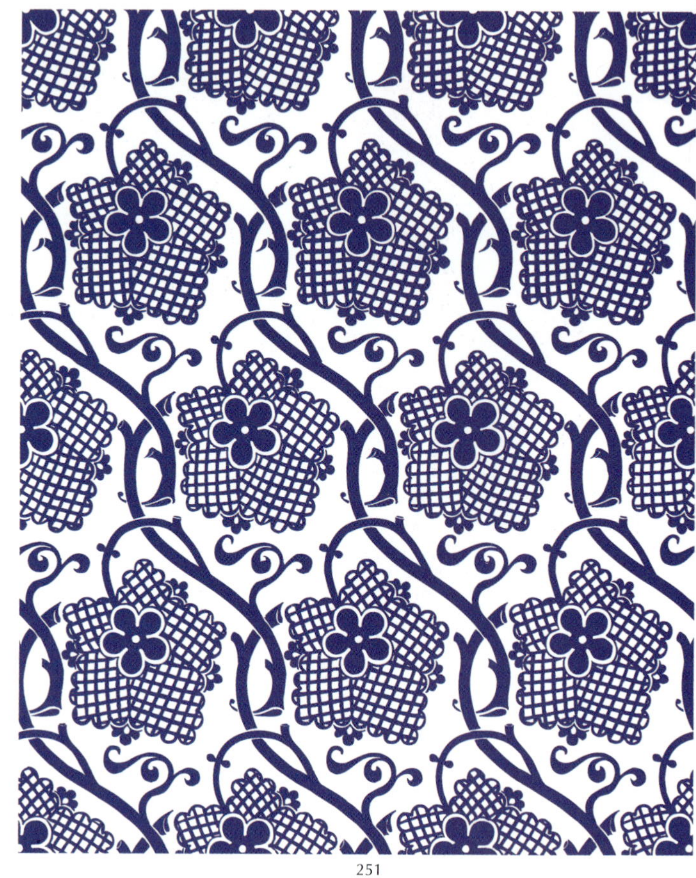

251

252

253

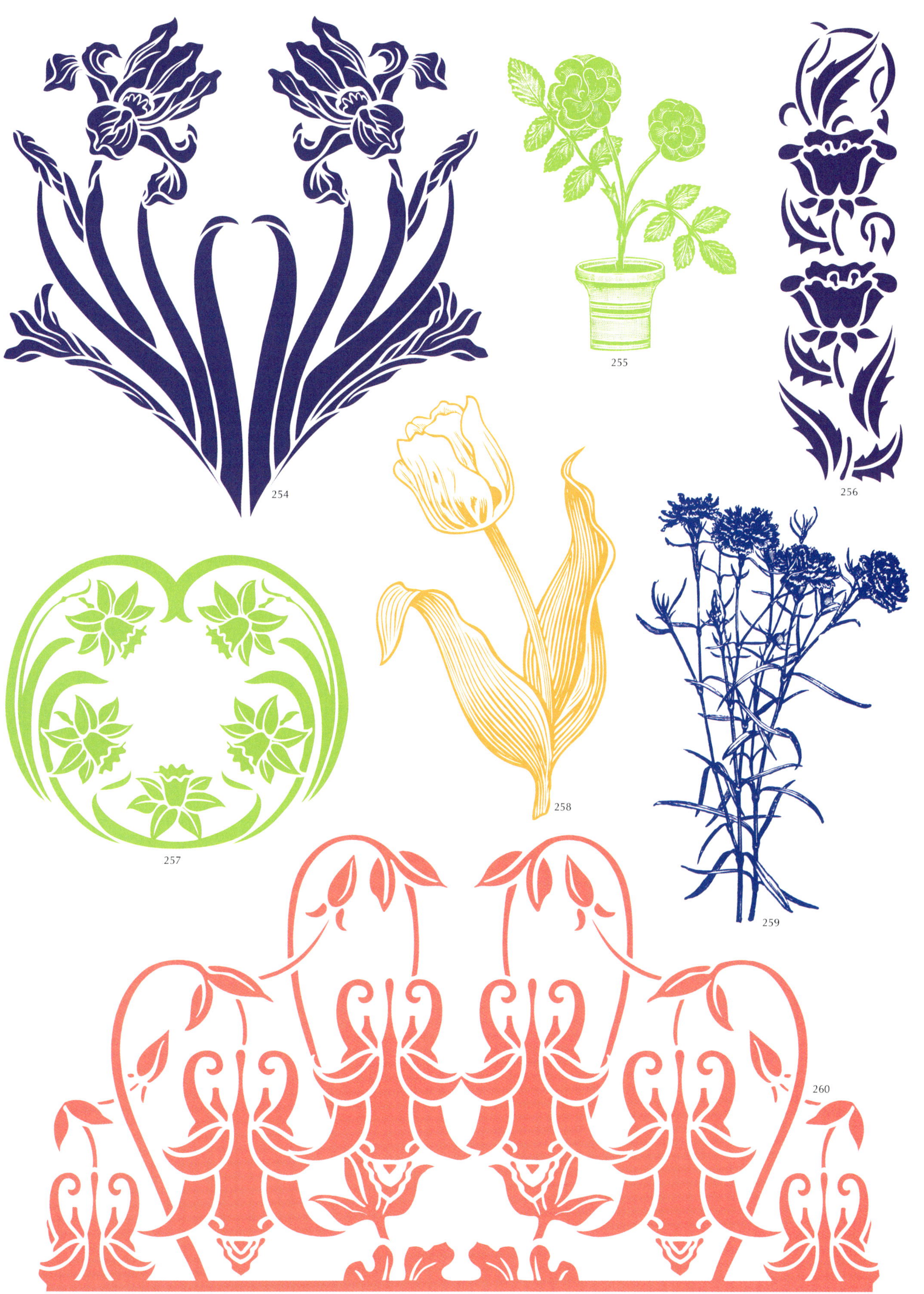
254
255
256
257
258
259
260

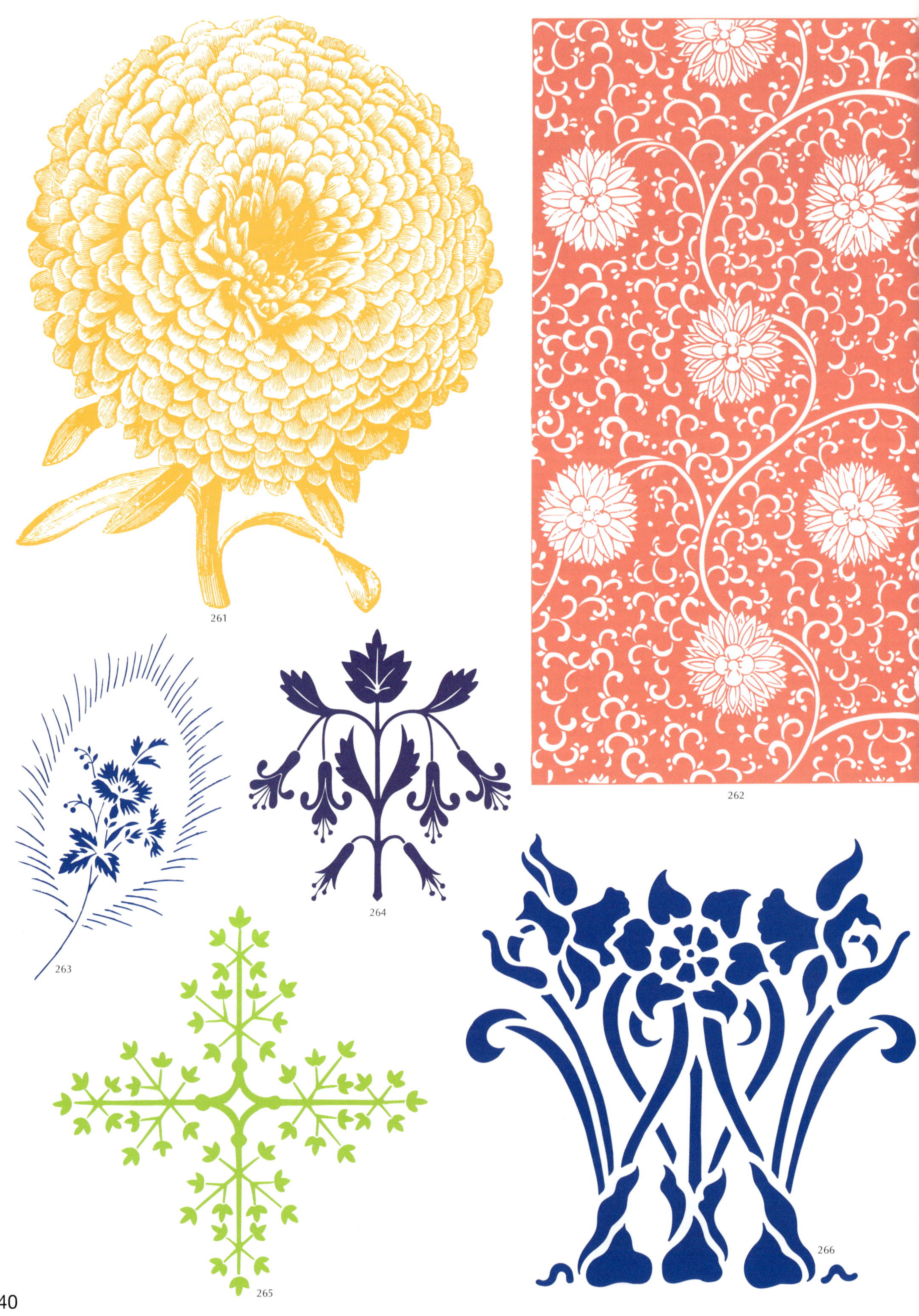

261

262

263

264

265

266

267
268
269
270
271
272
273
274

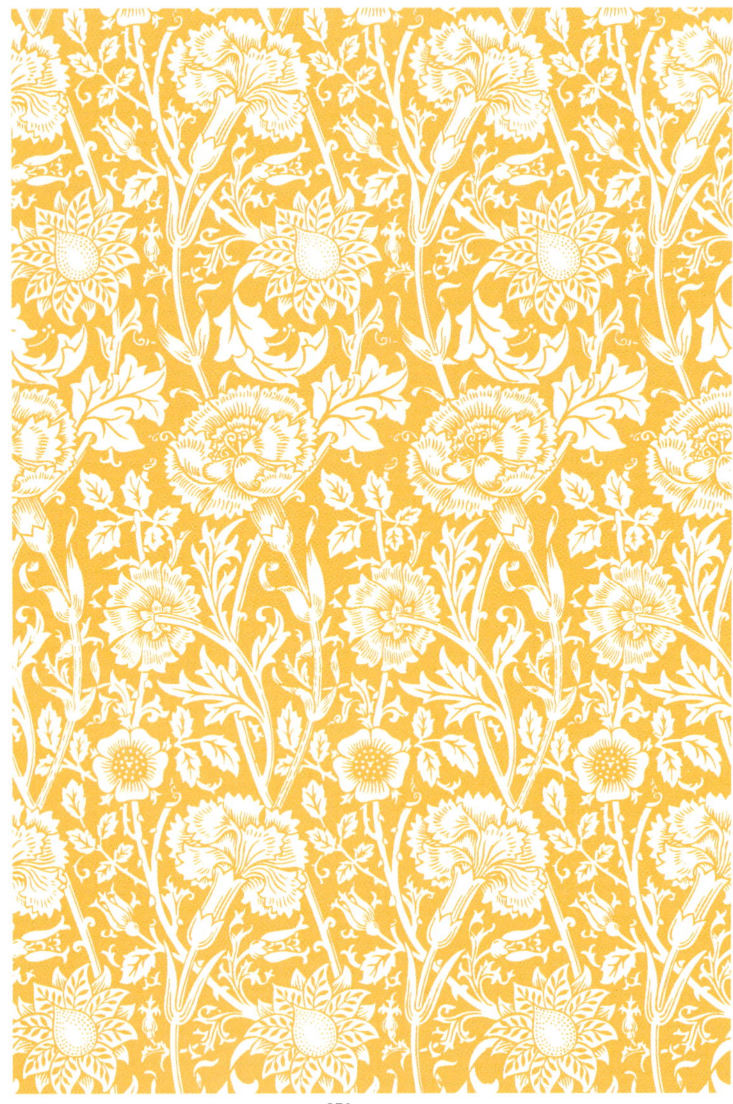

276

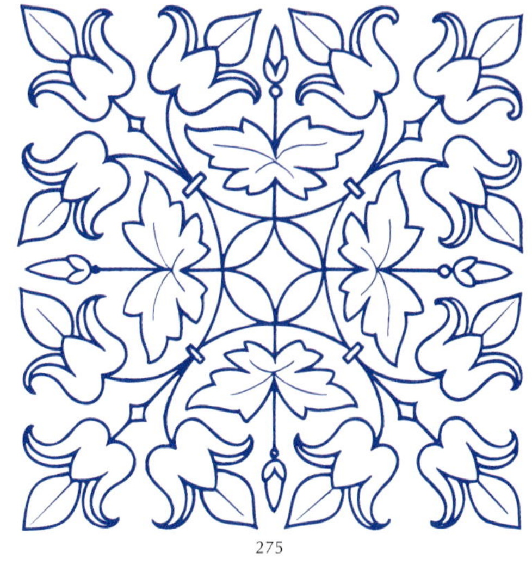

275

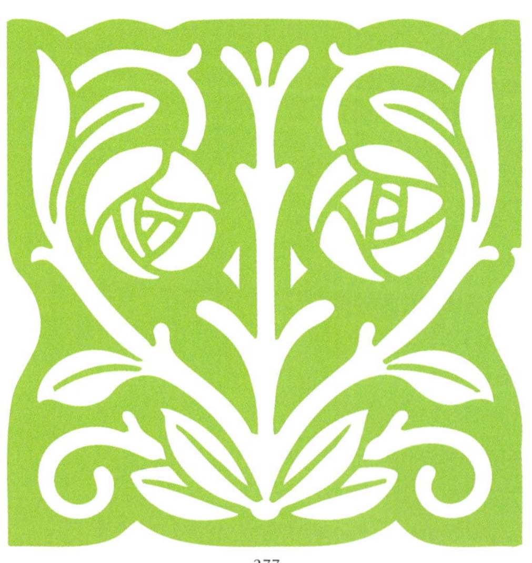

277

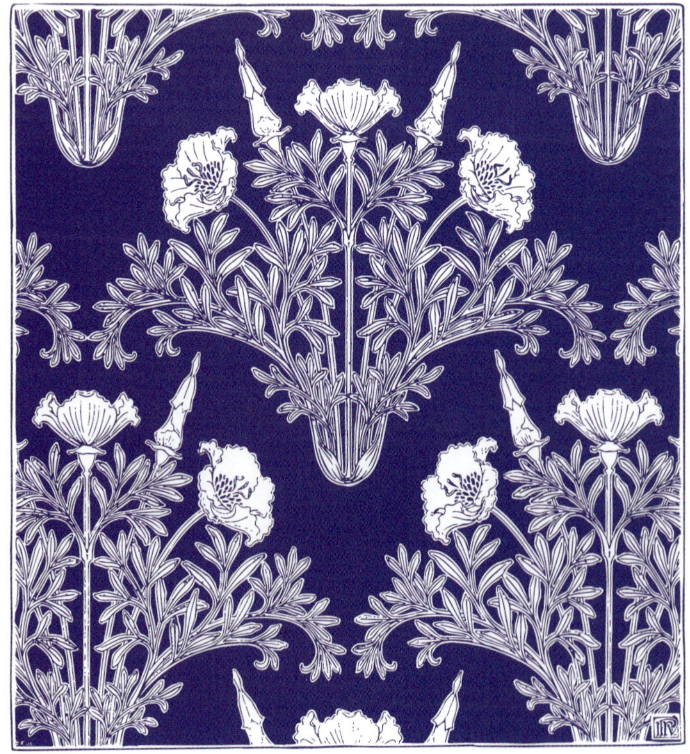

278

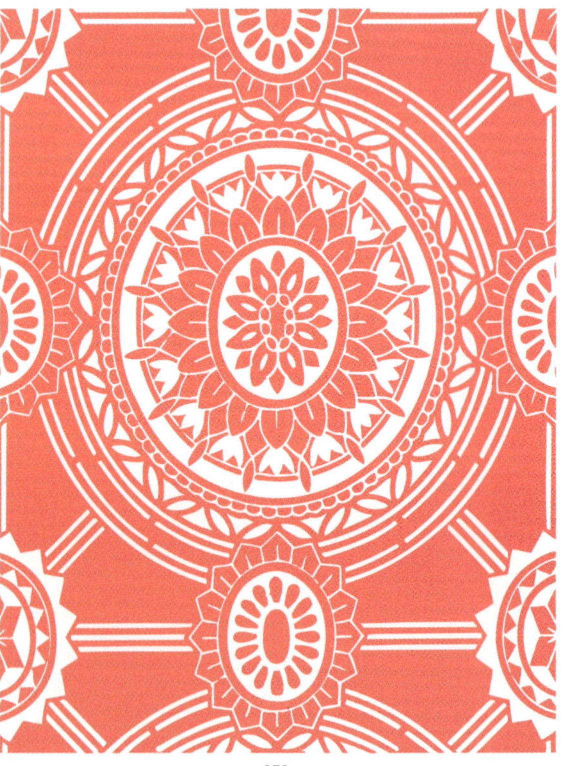

279

280

281

282

283

284

285

286

287

288

289

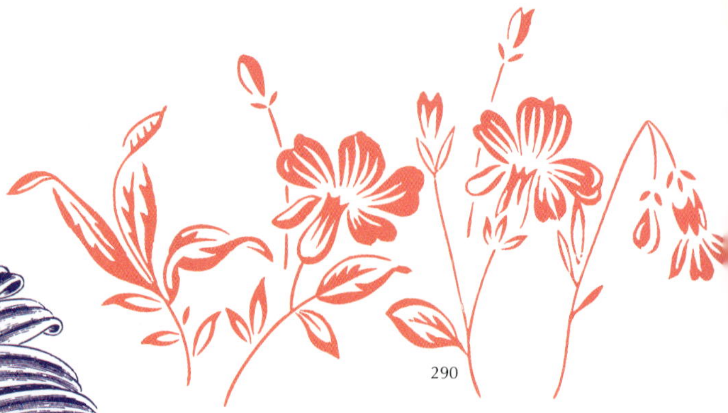

290

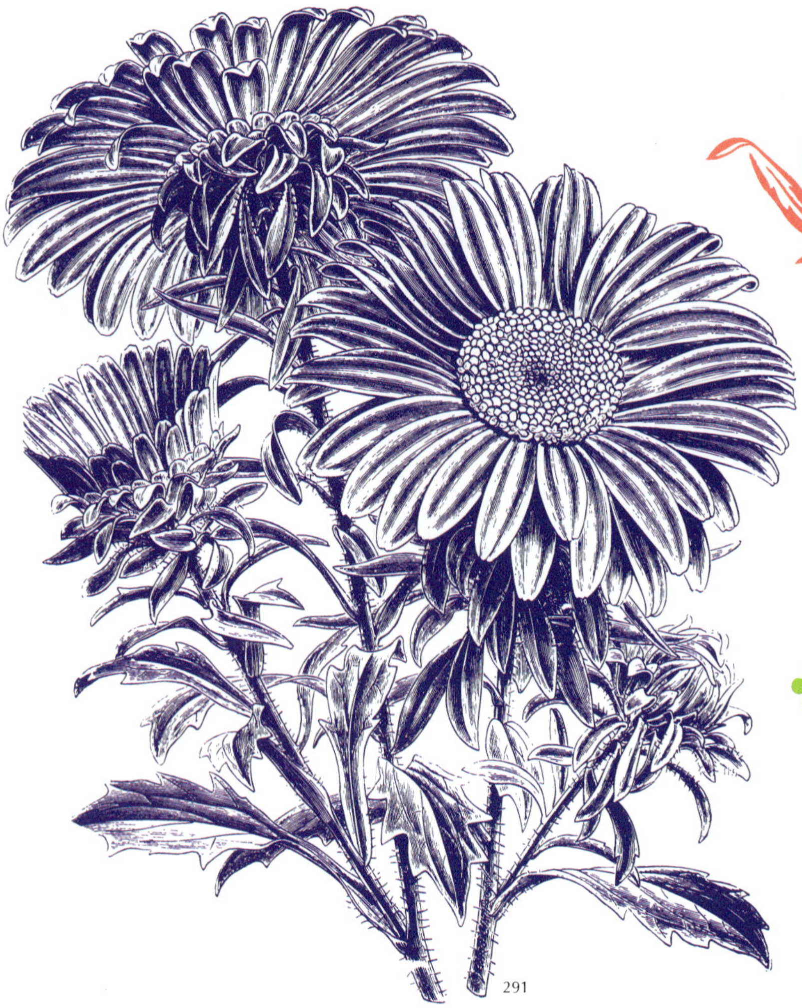

291

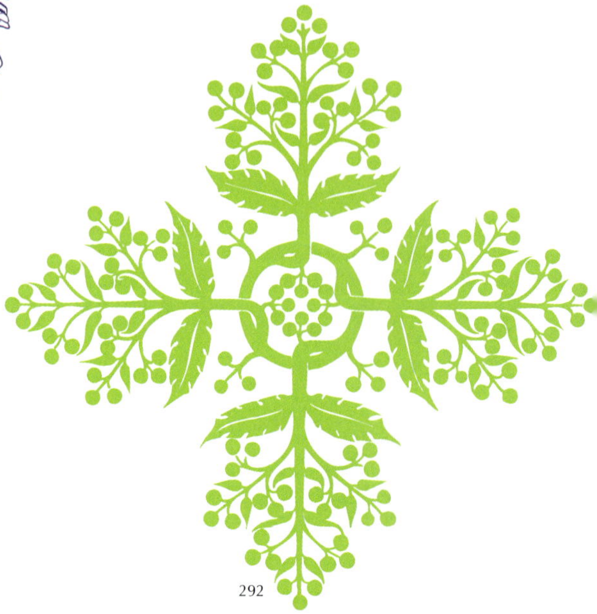

292

293

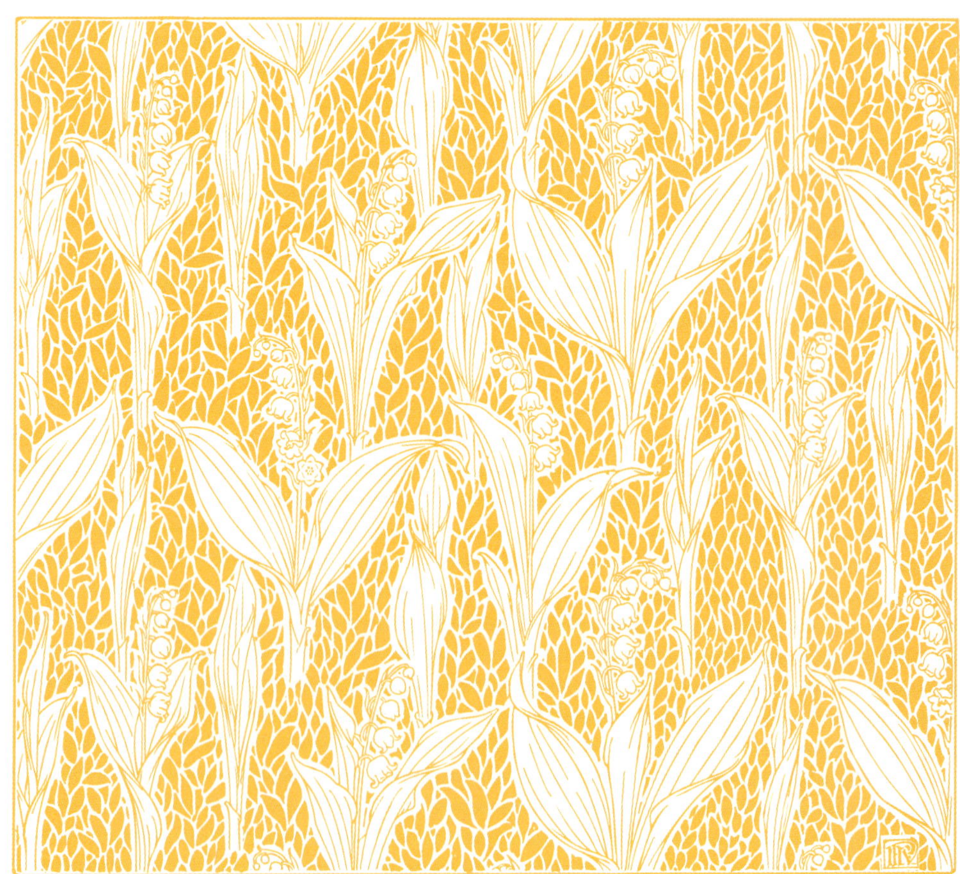

294

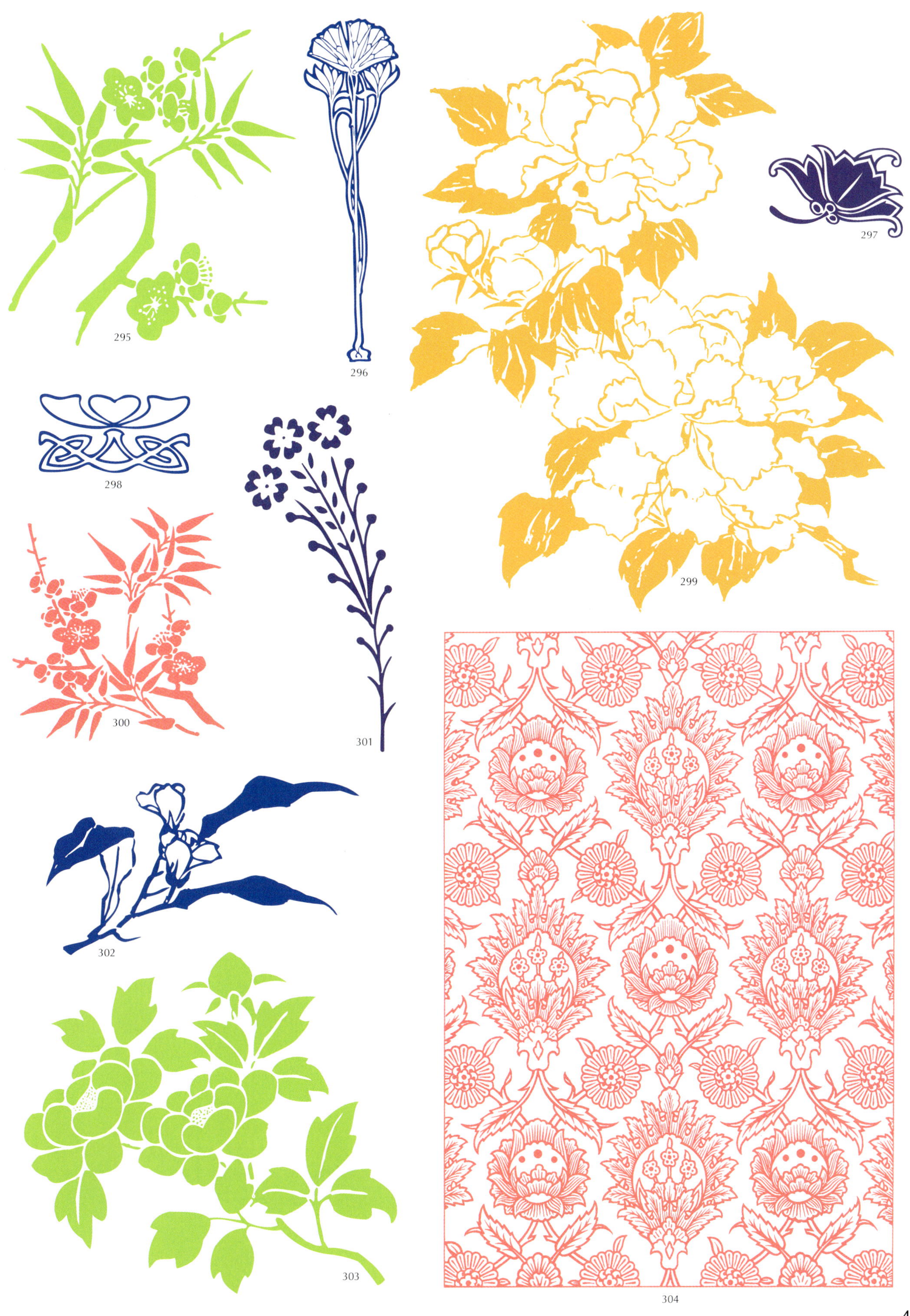
295
296
297
298
299
300
301
302
303
304